signotation

ASL WRITER'S GUIDE

How to Write Sign Language Using the 5 Parameters

S. Hansen CI/CT/SC:L/Ed:K-12

www.signotation.com

ISBN-13: 9780998718613
ISBN-10: 0998718610

DEDICATION

To the Deaf Community for their daily inspiration and kindness to me,
to bilingual Deaf and Hard of Hearing students
who are eager to learn new things
and to my family.

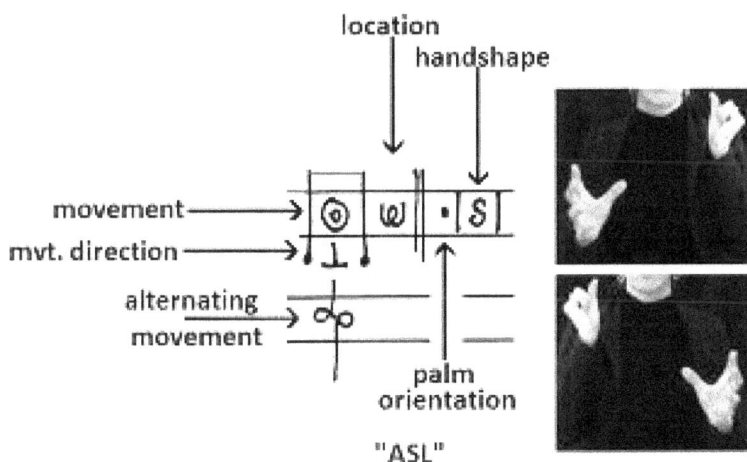

"ASL"

CONTENTS

ACKNOWLEDGMENTS...I

SIGNOTATION CORE PRINCIPLES 3

ACCESS TO ACADEMIC VOCABULARY 5

CONVENTIONS 8

THE 5 PARAMETERS..10

SIGNOTATION STAFF 11

BASIC SIGNOTATION..12

PARAMETER #1 HANDSHAPES....................................13

PARAMETER #2 PALM ORIENTATION 25

PARAMETER #3 LOCATION..34

PARAMETER #4 MOVEMENT..79

PARAMETER #5 FACIAL GRAMMAR 102

    P5 TYPE 1: SENTENCE TYPE......................................105

    P5 TYPE 2: FACIAL MORPHEMES.............................109

GRAMMAR NOTES...117

    ALTERNATING MVTS 118

    BASE HANDSHAPE PAIRS (BHS-P) 120

        BASE HANDSHAPE PAIRS: VERTICAL.....................121

        BASE HANDSHAPE PAIR VARIATIONS 123

BASE HANDSHAPE NUMERICAL INCORPORATION 125

BASE HANDSHAPE PAIRS: LATERAL 126

COMPOUND SIGNS 128

CONJUGATION OF VERBS 130

CROSS-OVER LOCATIONS 138

EMBEDDED MOVEMENTS 140

FINGERSPELLING, NUMBERS AND DATES................... 142

HANDSHAPE SHIFT................................ 143

HEAD NOD AND SHAKE 146

MIRROR MVTS................................ 146

PERSON-MARKER 148

PRONOUNS 150

PROXIMAL LOCATIONS 154

SEPARATION OF SIGNS IN A PHRASE 154

YES, NO 155

LISTING 156

SIGN-TO-TEXT ACADEMIC THESARUS 174

SPREAD THE SIGN: INTERNATIONAL SIGNS IN SIGNOTATION 210

WHAT ABOUT CLASSIFIERS/DEPICTING VERBS?............................ 212

THE 5 PARAMETERS SIGNOTATION CHARTS 214

S. HANSEN

ACKNOWLEDGMENTS

With gratitude to my family, the Deaf community and online viewers for their feedback, critique and encouragement to pursue further development of a structural approach to sign languages in a written form.

This project was inspired by the students and staff in the Pasco and Kennewick School Districts who are dedicated to bilingual literacy for each child. I absolutely love and am so honored to be a part of that learning process!

I have also been inspired by Dr. William Stokoe, whose work in the 1960s set an example of a person who sought out patterns and meaning independently based on interactional research in an irresistible quest to **explore, create and know.**

"BUTTERFLY"

SIGNOTATION CORE PRINCIPLES

"SIGNOTATION"

STRUCTURAL APPROACH: Signotation is a structural method of recording the simultaneous and consecutive aspects of ASL/signed languages. The sign staff has three tiers to organize the 5 Parameters.

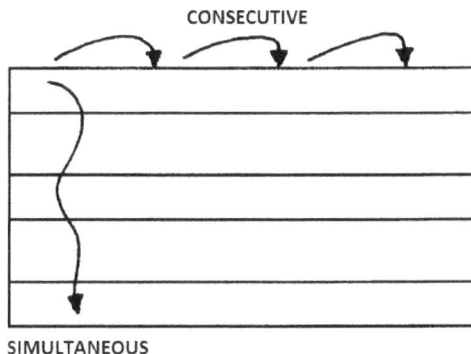

CONSECUTIVE

SIMULTANEOUS

ARBITRARY SYMBOLS: The notations and symbols used in signotation are arbitrary and can be changed and updated by the Deaf community and adapted to any sign language globally.

SHARED TOOL FOR BILINGUAL ED: Signotation is a "work in progress" and is offered as a possible tool to improve bilingual education and literacy of

Deaf/Hard of Hearing students and to increase awareness and appreciation of the structure and complexity of signed languages. Pragmatic uses include increased access to academic vocabulary, spelling, note-taking, and ASL as a second language applications. Students may experience increased retention and mastery of the elements of ASL via studying its written form.

SIGN BASED: All notations and symbols created are tied to actual signs in use.

ARTICULATION VARIANTS: A single "root" sign can have many articulations which reflect changes in meaning along with stylistic choices. For example, the root sign: "finish" can be articulated several ways, in different locations in the signing space to convey different meaning and intent. Signotation attempts to allow variations in articulation to be notated accurately.

INTERNAL COHESION: Notations are used consistently, ie: the notation for the palm as a location is also used for an open-palm sweep generic list.

COLLABORATIVE EFFORT: Writing a language is a shared community task. Signotation is a proposed approach to this task by an educational interpreter in the hopes that further study, research, experimentation, application and revision will generate a useful educational tool.

Standard Signing Spaces and Fingerspelling Space

ENHANCING LITERACY:
ACCESS TO ACADEMIC VOCABULARY
IN A "SIGN TO TEXT" THESARUS

One of the most exciting prospects about this approach, aside from the intrinsic value of interacting with and preserving your first language on paper, is the opportunity for students to utilize a "sign to text" thesaurus reference. This simple tool has the potential to increase access to academic terms independently by the student. Students frequently recall the first letter(s) of a term and would be able to scan and locate the desired term as well as learn new vocabulary. Signs with more than one articulation could be grouped together and nuances in meaning discussed. Here are a few examples of common academic terms.

"IMPORTANT"
"CRITICAL"
"VITAL"

"ANALYZE"
"ASSESSMENT"

"SECRET"
"PRIVATE"
"PASS" (WORD)
"CLANDESTINE"
"CONFIDENTIAL"

"MAKE"
"MANUFACTURE"
"PRODUCE"
"CREATE"

"BLOCK"
"PREVENT"
"BARRIER"
"OBSTACLE"
"THWART"

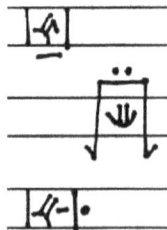

"ON THE FENCE"
"UNCERTAIN"
"INDECISIVE"
"AMBIVALENT"
"EQUIVOCATE"

"POLITE"
"COURTEOUS"
"MANNERS"

"LUCKY" / "LUCK"
"FORTUNATE"
"FORTUITOUS"

"EAT"
"HAVE A BITE TO EAT"
"CONSUME"
"MUNCH"
"INHALE"
"GOBBLE"
"SCARF IT DOWN"

"ILLEGAL"
"PROHIBITED"
"FORBIDDEN"
"UNLAWFUL"
"AGAINST THE RULES"

"SORRY"
"APOLOGIZE"
"REGRET"

CONVENTIONS

Signotation incorporates standard conventions including:

- alphabetical characters
- numerical characters and symbols
- punctuation marks and symbols
- musical and mathematical symbols

in conjunction with simple sketching and created symbols as needed for grammatically accurate detail.

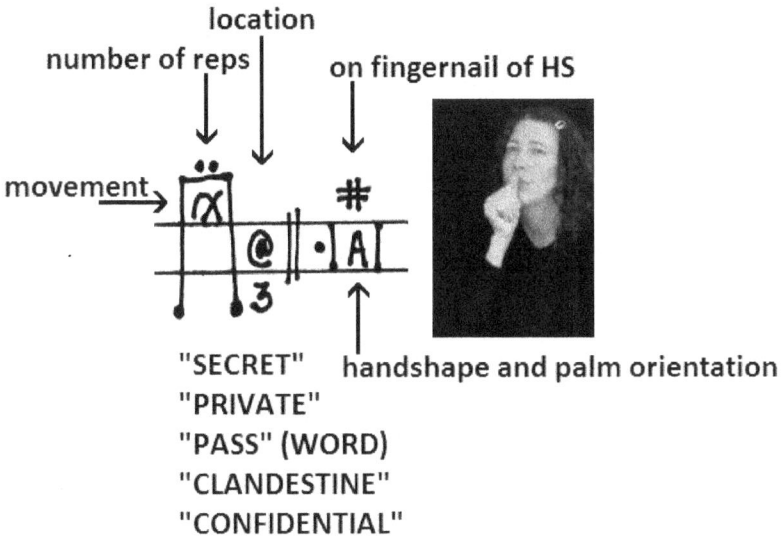

location

number of reps

on fingernail of HS

movement

"SECRET"   handshape and palm orientation
"PRIVATE"
"PASS" (WORD)
"CLANDESTINE"
"CONFIDENTIAL"

THE 5 PARAMETERS
OF SIGNOTATION ON THE SIGN STAFF

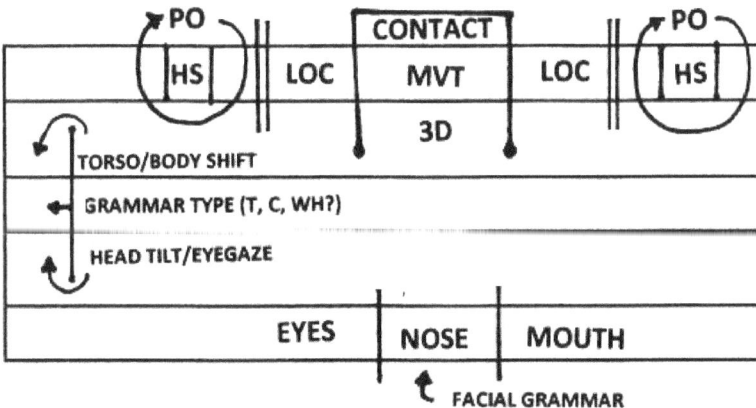

S. HANSEN

THE 5 PARAMETERS

1. Handshape (HS)

2. Palm Orientation (PO)

3. Location (LOC)

4. Movement (MVT)

5. Facial grammar (NMGM)

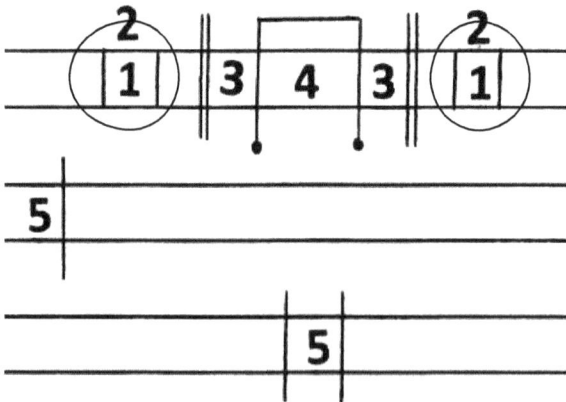

Source:
Linguistics of American Sign Language: An Introduction, Fifth Edition, 2011 by Valli, Lucas, Mulrooney and Villanueva (p. 21) "5 Parameters".

SIGNOTATION STAFF

Basic Signotation

The most basic notation will require 4 parameters: **Handshape (HS), Palm Orientation (PO), Location (LOC) and Movement (MVT)**.

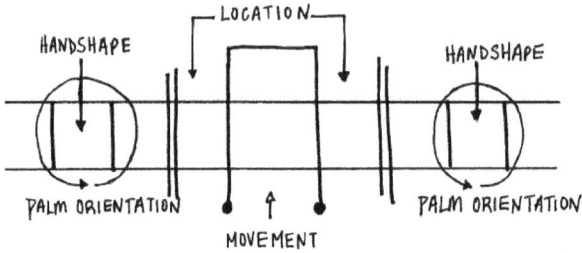

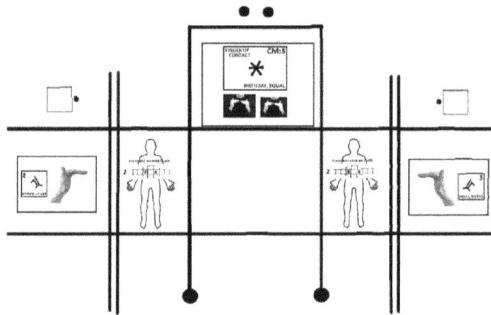

"EQUAL"

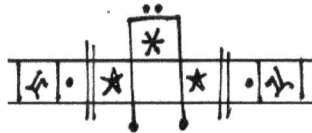

"EQUAL"

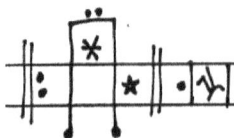

"EQUAL" (MIRROR NOTATION)

NOTE: The sign "equal" can be articulated in many ways, this is just one specific articulation. Each variation can also be notated.

PARAMETER #1
HANDSHAPES

handshape shift movement
and # of reps

1st handshape   2nd handshape

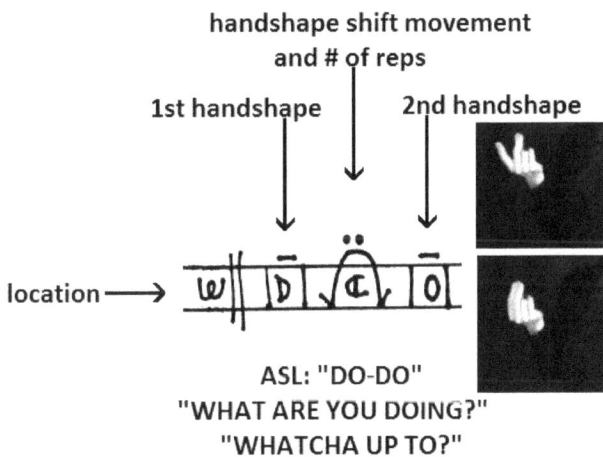

location ⟶

ASL: "DO-DO"
"WHAT ARE YOU DOING?"
"WHATCHA UP TO?"

HANDSHAPES

Many of the handshapes used in sign language are either

- **Alphabetical letters**

  or

- **Numbers**

We will use these handshapes along with a set of symbols to represent 57 more unique handshapes.

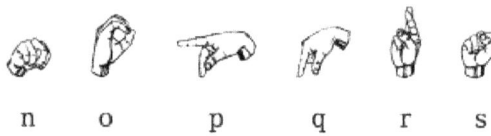

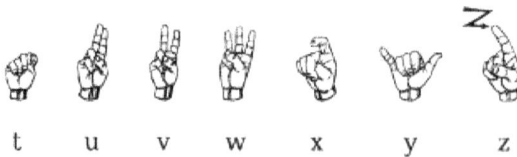

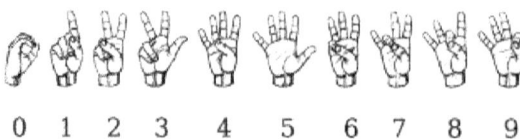

ORGANIZING SYMBOLS

In chemistry, the periodic table of the elements helps scientists around the globe organize the elements for easier visual access. We can borrow this method to design and categorize sign language parameter elements such as the handshapes, movements and facial grammar. The goal is a useful set of symbols that children can use in academic settings to enhance bilingualism and literacy.

Periodic Table of the Elements

H																	He
Li	Be											B	C	N	O	F	Ne
Na	Mg											Al	Si	P	S	Cl	Ar
K	Ca	Sc	Ti	V	Cr	Mn	Fe	Co	Ni	Cu	Zn	Ga	Ge	As	Se	Br	Kr
Rb	Sr	Y	Zr	Nb	Mo	Tc	Ru	Rh	Pd	Ag	Cd	In	Sn	Sb	Te	I	Xe
Cs	Ba	57-71	Hf	Ta	W	Re	Os	Ir	Pt	Au	Hg	Tl	Pb	Bi	Po	At	Rn
Fr	Ra	89-103	Rf	Db	Sg	Bh	Hs	Mt	Ds	Rg	Cn	Uut	Fl	Uup	Lv	Uus	Uuo

Lanthanide Series: La Ce Pr Nd Pm Sm Eu Gd Tb Dy Ho Er Tm Yb Lu

Actinide Series: Ac Th Pa U Np Pu Am Cm Bk Cf Es Fm Md No Lr

The following list is an example of handshapes and created symbols to represent those uniquely discernible handshapes along with sample sign references. A similar approach could be used for any sign language globally. Create a standard symbol to represent a specific, sign-bound handshape.

(P1) ASL SN HANDSHAPES CHART

1 BASE HANDSHAPE	1A	1B	1C	1D
2	3	4	5 C⁻	6
7 INDEX HANDSHAPE	8	9	10	11
12 ⊗	13 φ	14 ¢	15 X⁻	16 X⁺
17 8⁻	18 ⁼8	19 8⁺	20	21 A⁻
22 ₌5	23 0ˀ	24 ⁼O̅	25 N̄	26 N>
27 ₌2̂, V̄	28 N⁻	29 ⁼L̄	30 H⁻	31
32	33	34 R	35 R⁻	36 R
37 Y3	38 Y1	39 F̄	40 F>	41 5
42 5̂	43 Ĉ	44 53	45 4̂	46 3̂
47 2̂	48 1̂	49 5⁻	50 9⁻	51 7⁻
52 6⁻	53 2ˀ	54 3ˀ		

16

(P1) CLOSE-UP

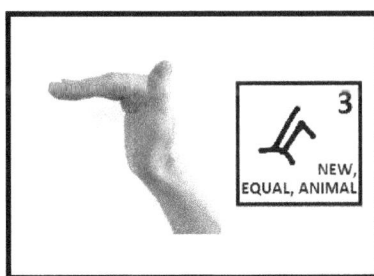

1
SCHOOL, COOK
BASE HANDSHAPE

1A
RELAXED BHS (DOWNWARD)

1B
RELAXED BHS (UPWARD)

1C
ARMS CRADLE
BHS: DAUGHTER, SON

1D
HANDS CRADLE
BHS: BABY

2
HAMBURGER

3
NEW, EQUAL, ANIMAL

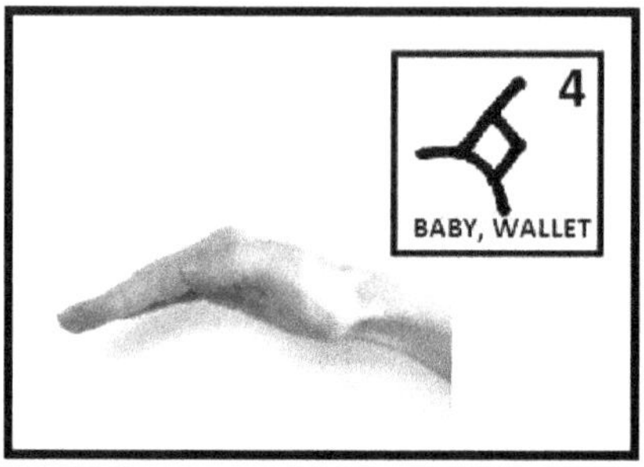

4 — BABY, WALLET

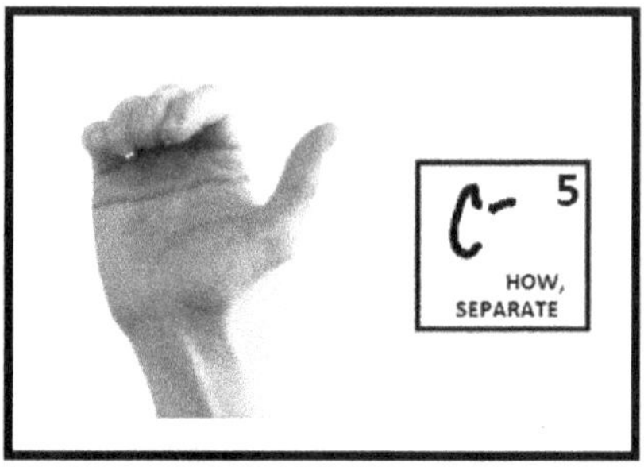

5 — HOW, SEPARATE

6 — DOLLAR, AMMENDMENT

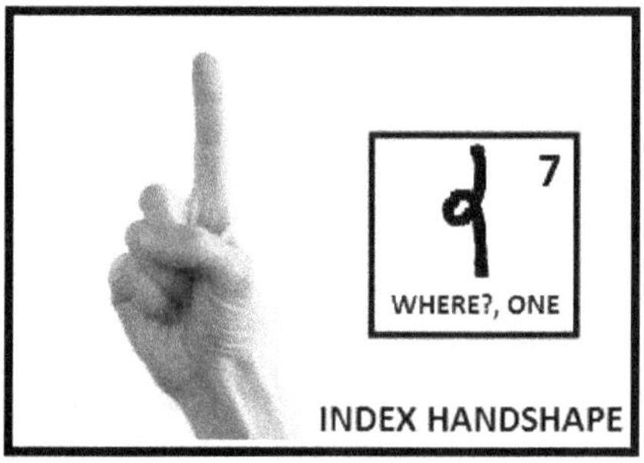

7 — WHERE?, ONE

INDEX HANDSHAPE

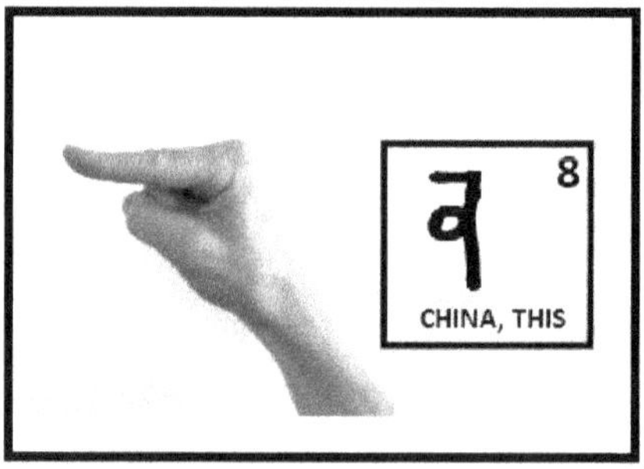

8 — CHINA, THIS

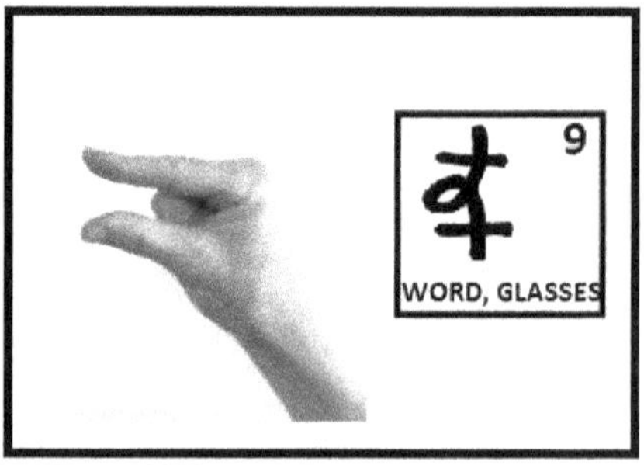

9 — WORD, GLASSES

10 — OPEN BIRD BEAK

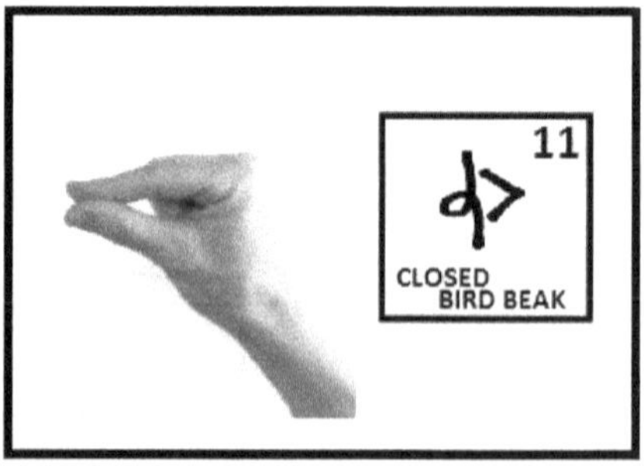

11 — CLOSED BIRD BEAK

⊗ 12
WRITE, DETAILS

φ 13
PIERCED EAR

¢ 14
MOON, PLATE

X⁻ 15
WHO, RUN

X⁺ 16
TURN CHANNEL

8⁻ 17
HS SOPH
FEEL, INTERNET

8̿ 18
LIKE (FT 1)

8⁺ 19
AWFUL, HATE

20
AWFUL,
HATE (PT 2)

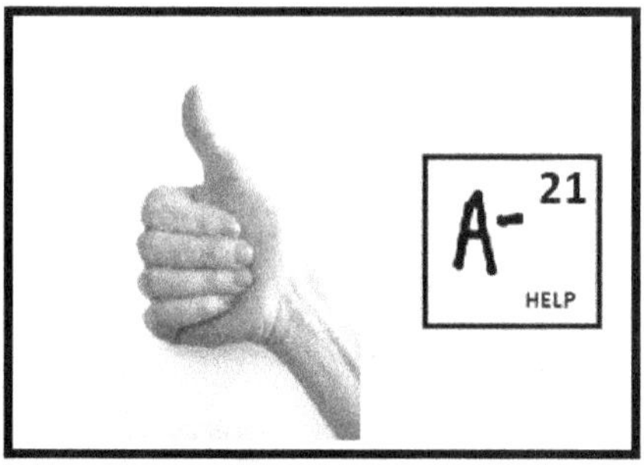
21
HELP

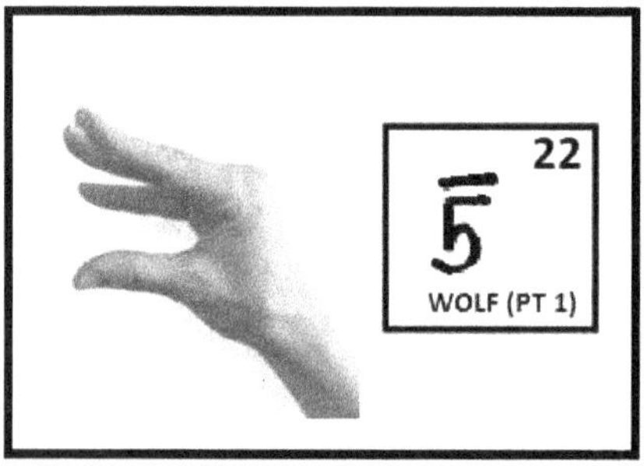
22
WOLF (PT 1)

23
TEACH,
MORE

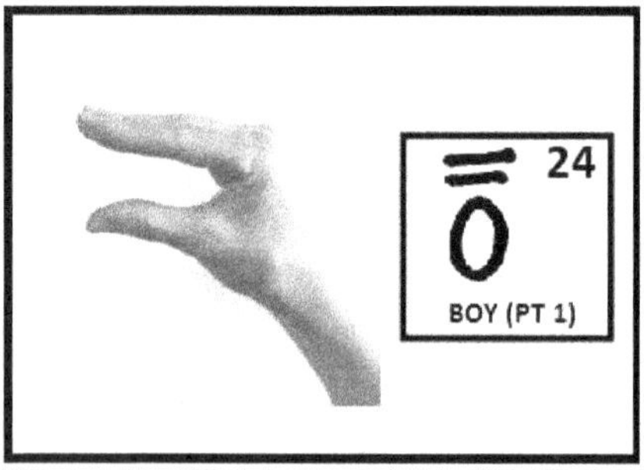
24
BOY (PT 1)

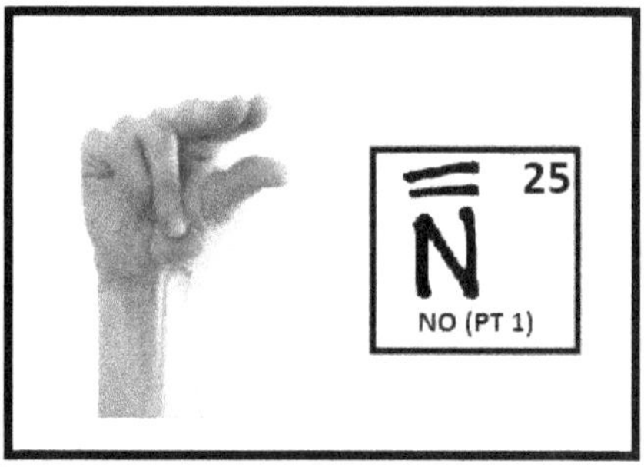
25
NO (PT 1)

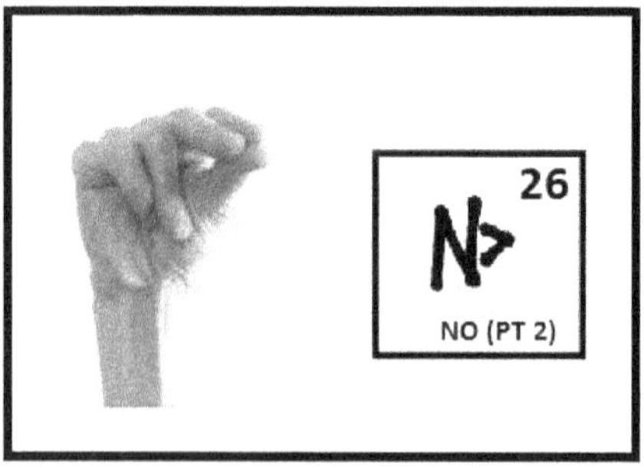
26
NO (PT 2)

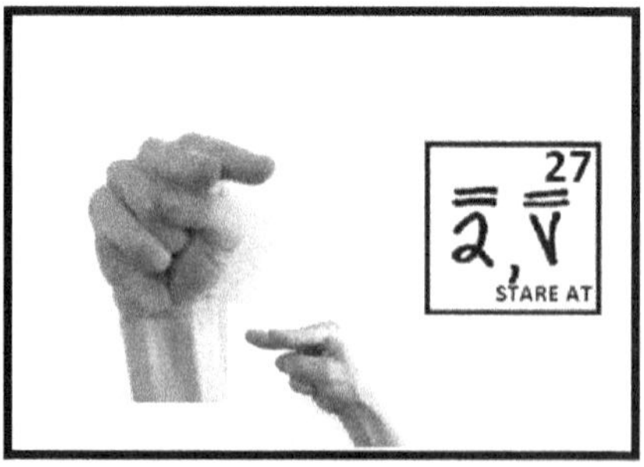
27
STARE AT

N- **28** FUNNY, CUTE, BUTTER		$\overline{\overline{L}}$ **29** WELDING	
H- **30** GUN, INNOCENT		ʰrᵛ **31** I LOVE YOU	
ʰrᵛ **32** KID, CELLPHONE		ʰrᵛ> **33** CHIHUAHUA	
Rᵛ **34** I REALLY LOVE U		R- **35** DOLPHIN	

R 36
RULE, RESTAURANT

Y3 37
FINGERSPELL

Y1 38
PILOT (PT 1)

F̃ 39
CAT (PT 1), RING

F> 40
PREACH AT

5 41
WHAT?, MASK

5 42
WANT, BALL

C 43
COOKIE, CHERISH (PT 1)

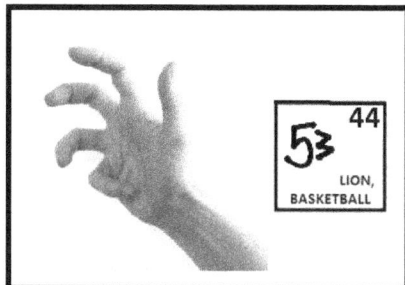

44
5₃
LION,
BASKETBALL

45
ᴹ4
COMB (HAIR)

46
ᴹ3
INVEST $

47
ᴹ2
BLIND

48
ᴹ↑
GLASS

49
5⁻
HS SR

50
9⁻
HS JUNIOR

51
7⁻
HS FRESHMAN

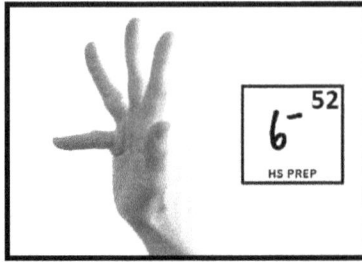

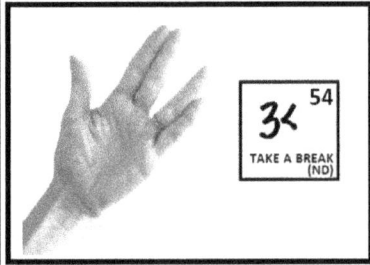

PARAMETER #2
PALM ORIENTATION

(P2) ASL SN PALM ORIENTATION CHART

BASIC PO (R,L,F,B)   ANGLED PO

PO down to the ground: "CHILD"

PO Up to the sky: "MAYBE"

PO TO THE MIDLINE   PO SETTING 1   PO SETTING 2

FINGERTIP DIRECTION

fingertips angled inward   fingertips angled outward

45 DEGREE TILT

(P2) CLOSE-UP

VERTICAL PALM ORIENTATION (VPO)

VPO is marked by a dot on the outside perimeter of the HS block:

BASIC PO (R,L,F,B)   ANGLED PO

Examples:

PO back: "MY"

"MY"

PO forward: "YOUR"

"YOUR"

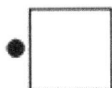

PO left: "MOTHER"

27

PO angled: "NAME"

HORIZONTAL PALM ORIENTATION (HPO)

HPO is marked by a solid line below or above the HS block:

PO down to the ground: "CHILD"

PO Up to the sky: "MAYBE"

PALM ORIENTATION: SETTINGS

The default orientation of a handshape is based on its **alphabetical position**. Since the wrist can rotate but still have the same palm orientation, we need to notate the wrist rotation. When the palm orientation stays the same but the handshape has rotated we can notate these shifts in settings, which rotate clockwise.

PO TO THE MIDLINE

"MORE"
P.O. TO THE MIDLINE

"DATE"
P.O. TO THE MIDLINE

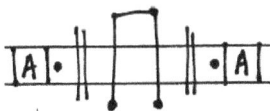

"PURSE"
P.O. TO THE MIDLINE

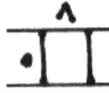

PO SETTING 1

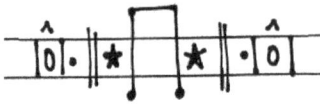

"MORE"
P.O. SETTING 1

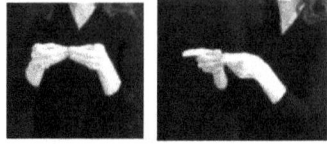

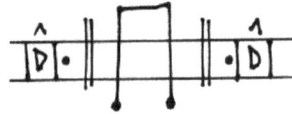

"DESSERT"
P.O. SETTING 1

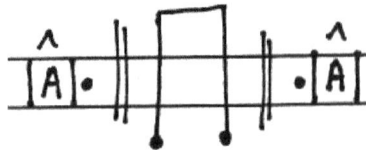

"WITH"
P.O. SETTING 1

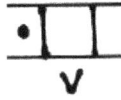

PO SETTING 2

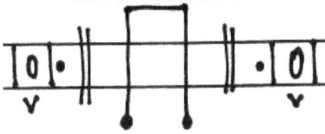

"OVARIES"
P.O. SETTING 2

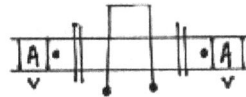

"CRUTCHES"
P.O. SETTING 2

COMBINATION PO (MIDLINE AND SETTING 2)

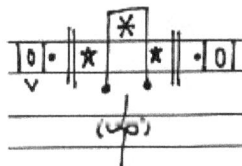

"NUMBER"
P.O. MIDLINE AND
SETTING 2
ALTERNATING MVT

(a lateral alternating HS caused by the rotation of the PO)

FINGERTIP DIRECTION

The default for handshape fingertip direction is pointing forward away from the signer, or upward towards the sky.

default fingertips forward   **default fingertips upward**

The fingertip direction is related to palm orientation and settings. It may be helpful or at times necessary to notate the fingertip directions using a simple "tic" mark for angled handshapes such as the sign for name:

fingertips angled inward   **fingertips angled outward**

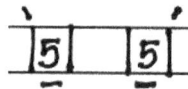

"NAME"

without fingertip mark

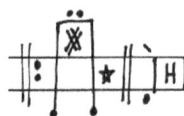

"NAME"

with fingertip mark

45 DEGREE TILT

Some signs have a slanted PO. An upward or downward tilt in fingertip orientation from the "sky" or "ground" PO is notated using a combination of the palm orientations:

"MIRROR"

PARAMETER #3
LOCATION

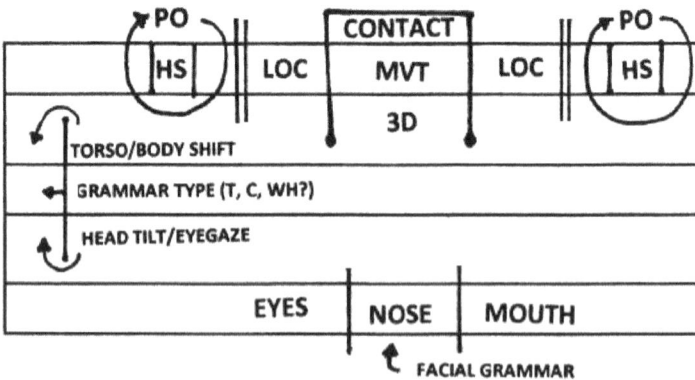

"HOUSE"

(P3) ASL SN LOCATIONS CHART

6 BASIC LOCATIONS:

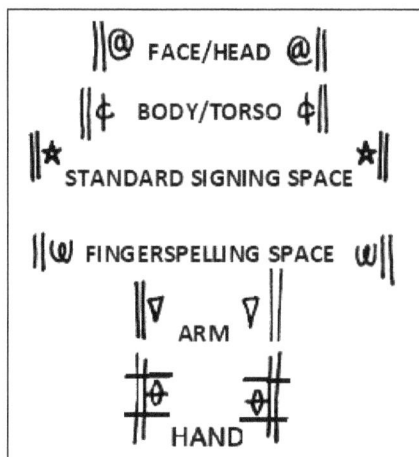

‖@ , ‖¢ , ‖★ , ‖ω , ‖▽ , ‖θ

‖@ FACE/HEAD @‖
‖¢ BODY/TORSO ¢‖
‖★ STANDARD SIGNING SPACE ★‖
‖ω FINGERSPELLING SPACE ω‖
‖▽ ARM ▽‖
#θ HAND #θ

‖@ FACE/HEAD LOCATIONS @‖

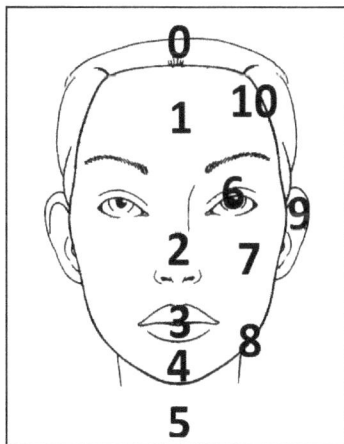

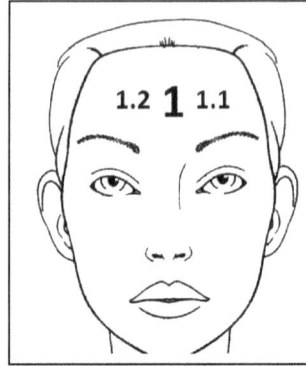

0
0/2   0.1

1.2 **1** 1.1

2.5
2.4 **2** 2.3
2.2 2.6 2.1

3.2 3.1
3> **3** <3

3.1 and 3.2 = corners of mouth
<3 and 3> = sides of mouth ie:
"RESTAURANT"

3.3 Upper lip
3.5 Upper teeth
3.7 Edge of upper teeth
3.8 Open mouth
3.6 Lower teeth
3.4 Lower lip
3.9 Tongue

4.2 **4** 4.1
4.3

5.3
5.2 **5** 5.1
5.4

6

6.4
6.2
6.5
6.1 6.3
6.6

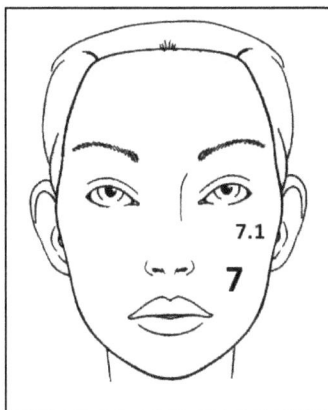

7.1
7

9.2
9.3
9
9.1 9.4
9.5

9.6 Behind the ear

8.1
8

10

||¢ TORSO LOCATIONS ¢||

30		20
3	2	1
6	5	4
9	8	7
12	11	10

VERTICAL LOCATIONS #1-5

Standard Signing Spaces
and Fingerspelling Space

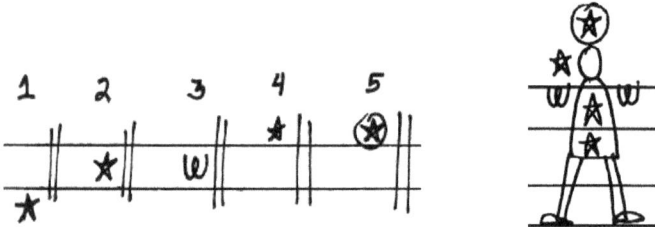

LATERAL LOCATIONS

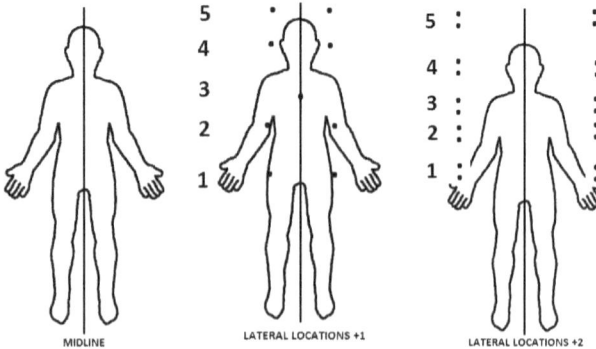

MIDLINE

LATERAL LOCATIONS +1

LATERAL LOCATIONS +2

38

HORIZONTAL LOCATIONS

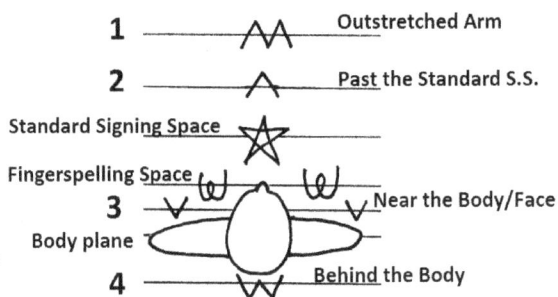

1 —————— Outstretched Arm

2 —————— Past the Standard S.S.

Standard Signing Space

Fingerspelling Space

3 —————— Near the Body/Face

Body plane

4 —————— Behind the Body

SIDE LOCATION

ARMPIT LOCATION

HIP LOCATION

ADDITIONAL BODY LOCATIONS

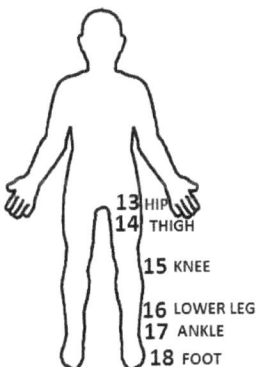

13 HIP
14 THIGH
15 KNEE
16 LOWER LEG
17 ANKLE
18 FOOT

39

THE ARM AND HAND

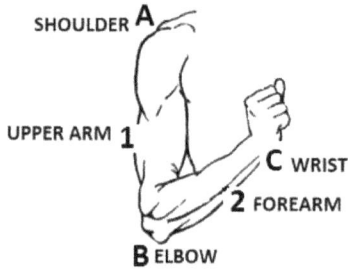

ARM , **HAND**

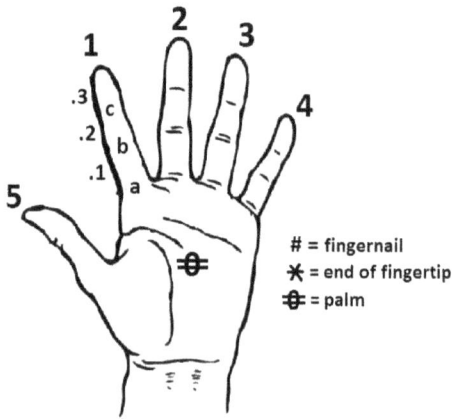

SHOULDER **A**

UPPER ARM **1**

C WRIST

2 FOREARM

B ELBOW

HAND AND FINGER IDENTIFICATION

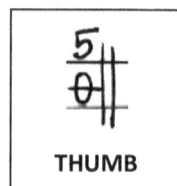

= fingernail
✳ = end of fingertip
⊕ = palm

FINGER LOCATION

THUMB

THE PALM

NON DOMINANT   DOMINANT

TOP SURFACE OF THE PALM (Back of the hand) IE: "WARRANT"

INSIDE EDGE OF ND PALM   IE: "MEAT"

THE FOUR FACES OF THE ARM

"DUTY" LOC   "DOCTOR" LOC

"CYST ON WRIST" (INSIDE)   "CYST ON WRIST" (OUTSIDE)

(P3) CLOSE-UP

THE 3-DIMENSIONS OF ASL

1D ✛ VERTICAL

2D ⊶ LATERAL

3D ≢ HORIZONTAL

6 BASIC LOCATIONS:

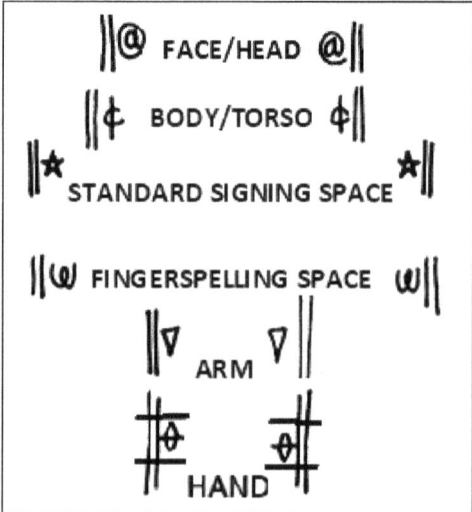

‖@ , ‖¢ , ‖★ , ‖ω , ‖▽ , ‖θ

‖@ FACE/HEAD @‖

‖¢ BODY/TORSO ¢‖

‖★ STANDARD SIGNING SPACE ★‖

‖ω FINGERSPELLING SPACE ω‖

‖▽ ARM ▽‖

‖θ HAND θ‖

Note: Locations are sites of contact unless otherwise noted as proximal.

FACE/HEAD LOCATIONS
PRIMARY

FACE/HEAD LOCATIONS
SECONDARY

CROWN

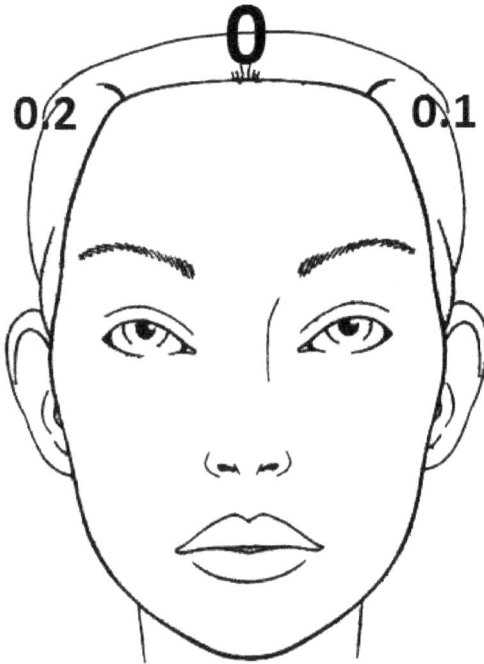

SAMPLES:

0 = "hat"
.2 = "lettuce"
.1 and .2 = "deer"

FOREHEAD

SAMPLES:

1 = "smart", "hearing" (attitude)
1.1 - 1.2 = "forget"

NOSE

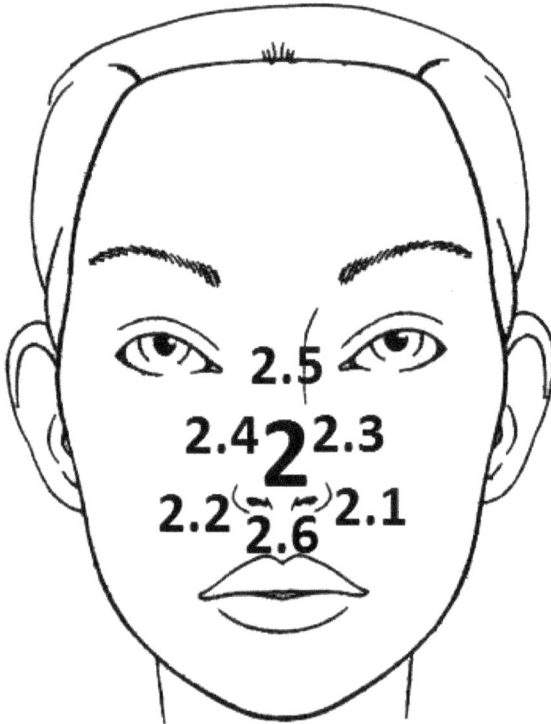

SAMPLES:

2 = "mouse"
2.1 - 2.2 = "flower"
2.1 and 2.2 = "boring"
2.1 - 2.2 = "deaf-nose" (can't smell)
2.3 or 2.4 "brown-nose"
2.5 = "nerd"
2.6 = "kid"

MOUTH

3.1 and 3.2 = corners of mouth
<3 and 3> = sides of mouth ie:
"RESTAURANT"

3.3 Upper lip
3.5 Upper teeth
3.7 Edge of upper teeth
3.8 Open mouth
3.6 Lower teeth
3.4 Lower lip
3.9 Tongue

SAMPLES:

3 = "talk", "shhh"
3.1 - 3.2 = "zip lips"
3.2 = "water, lemon"
3.3 = "apply lipstick"
3.4 = "red", "hearing", "taste"
3.5 = "glass"
3.6 = "lower teeth"
3.7 = "nut"
3.8 = "sucks"
3.9 = "stick your tongue out"

CHIN

SAMPLES:

4 = "favorite", "who", "orange"
4.1 and 4.2 = "honeymoon"
4.2 = "mother/mama"
4.3 = "not", "dirty"

NECK

5.3

5.2 **5** 5.1

5.4

SAMPLES:

5 = "turn off voice"
5.1 - 5.2 = "thyroid" or "choke on car"
5.3 - 5.4 = "thirsty"

EYE

SAMPLES:

6 = "eye", "contacts" (part 2), "pirate"
6.1 = "inside corner of eye"
6.2 = "eye lid"
6.3 = "outer corner of eye"
6.4 = "black"
6.5 = "Dad"
6.6 = "cry", "tears", "seeing is proof/witness"

CHEEKS

SAMPLES:

7 = "cat", "candy", "home" (pt.2)
7.1 = "see" (cheekbone)

JAW

SAMPLES:

8 = "tomorrow", "wife", "sister"
8.1 = "wisdom teeth",
8.1 - 8 = "girl"

EAR

9.6 Behind the ear

SAMPLES:

9 = "listen with ears", "the ear"
9.1 - 4 = "deaf"
9.2 = "hearing aid"
9.3 = "top of the ear"
9.4 = "ear mold"
9.5 = "foul"
9.6 = "cochlear implant"

TEMPLE

SAMPLES:

10 = "Father", "mind/think", "common sense", "cow", "horse"

SAMPLE SIGN LOCATIONS: FACE/HEAD

"DEAF"

"HARD OF HEARING"

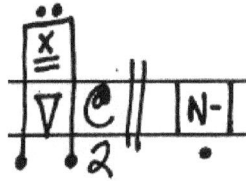

"FUNNY"
"AMUSING"

"CUTE"
"DARLING"
"ADORABLE"

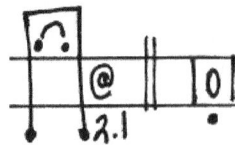

"FLOWER"
"POSY"

TORSO LOCATIONS

30		20
3	2	1
6	5	4
9	8	7
12	11	10

"WHAT'S UP"

(MIRROR MOVEMENT NOTATION)

1D ✟ VERTICAL LOCATIONS #1-5

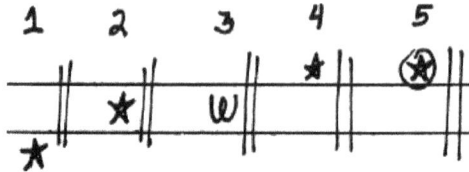

The **vertical plane** is the first dimension. There are five main sections or zones that exist for the signer vertically. Each is approximately a handbreadth apart. These locations are:

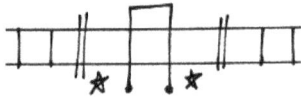

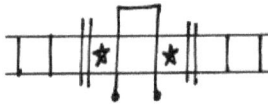

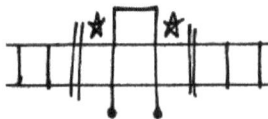

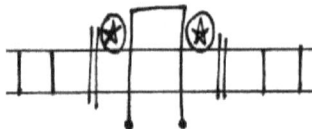

VERTICAL LOCATION #1

VERTICAL LOCATION #2
(STANDARD SIGNING SPACE)

STANDARD SIGNING SPACE

2

STANDARD SIGNING SPACE

Standard Signing Space
overhead view

VERTICAL LOCATION #3
(FINGERSPELLLING LOCATION)

VERTICAL LOCATION #4

VERTICAL LOCATION #5

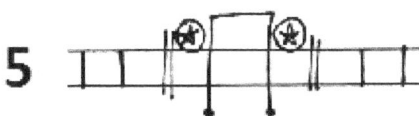

2D ✛ LATERAL LOCATIONS

The **midline or lateral plane** is the second dimension. There are three main sections or zones that exist for the signer symmetrically based on the midline. Each is approximately a handbreadth apart. These locations are:

- o THE MIDLINE (default vertical position except for fingerspelling location)

- o LATERAL LOCATION +1 (the side or arm section)
  Note: the fingerspelling location moves to the midline

- o LATERAL LOCATION +2 (The outer region, beyond the perimeter of the body)

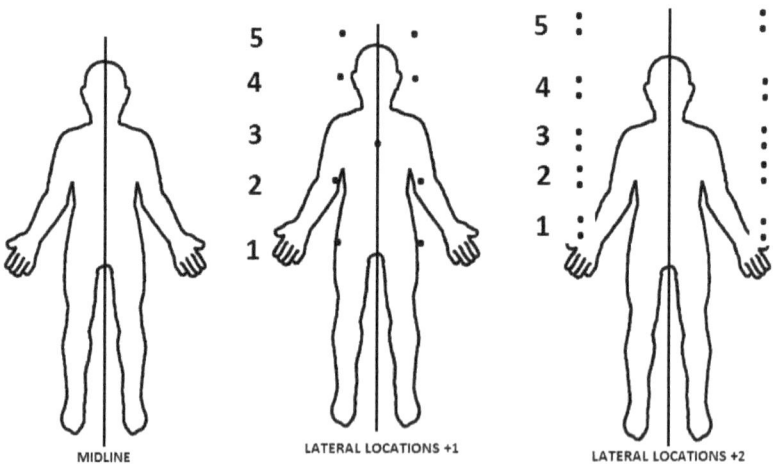

MIDLINE

LATERAL LOCATIONS +1

LATERAL LOCATIONS +2

SAMPLE SIGN LOCATIONS:

NOTE: The following sign locations are for demonstration purposes and particular signs can be moved to different locations and notated accordingly. For example, the sign "play" can also be signed over the head, in the standard signing space, or lower in vertical location #1, and signed with one or both hands.

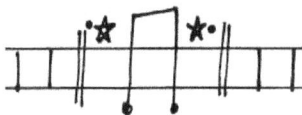

"YAY HANDS WAVING" LOC

"BASKETBALL"

"PLAY" LOC

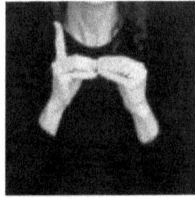

"ONE MORE" LOC

SUBDIVIDING LOCATIONS:

To subdivide a location, you can use the directional notations for up, down, right, left etc... and use a comma to show the specific locations. For example the signs for "the same" and "shoe" occur in the left and right hand sections of the standard signing space:

"SHOE"

3D ✚ HORIZONTAL LOCATIONS

The **horizontal plane** is the third dimension. Movements forward or back add the final layer of spatial detail. The 3-D aspect for the standard signing space, fingerspelling and the body plane are embedded. Below are the remaining 4 areas of the horizontal plane:

Here is a more detailed look at that set of locations:

1	ᴧᴧ	**Outstretched Arm**
2	ᴧ	**Past the Standard S.S.**
Standard Signing Space	☆	
Fingerspelling Space	ω	
3	ᴠ ω ω	**Near the Body/Face**
Body plane		
4	ᴡ	**Behind the Body**

SAMPLE SIGN LOCATIONS:

NOTE: The following sign locations are for demonstration purposes and particular signs can be moved to different locations and notated accordingly.

"WHERE" LOC

PERSON WALKS UP FROM RIGHT REAR TO FINGERSPELLING SPACE

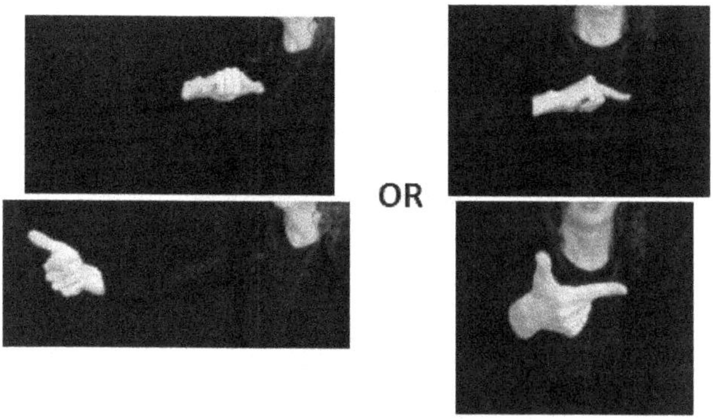

OR

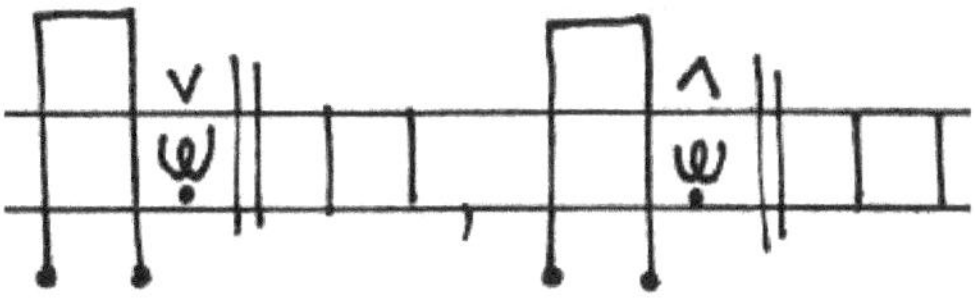

"MY TURN, YOUR TURN" LOC

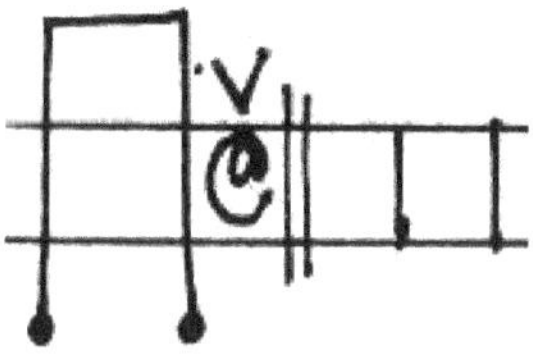

"SILLY" LOC
"RIDICULOUS"

"AFRAID" LOC
"SCARED"
"FRIGHTENED"

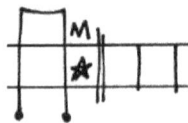

"WAIT" LOC

"TIME" (2)

"TIME" (2)
FORWARD LOCATION

(BASE HANDSHAPE PAIR)

SIDE LOCATION

The side of the torso, for example the sign: "monkey".

"MONKEY" LOC

71

ARMPIT LOCATION

The armpit, for example the sign: "animal".

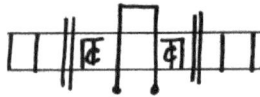

"ANIMAL" LOC

HIP LOCATION

The hip, for example the sign: "tail wagging".

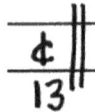

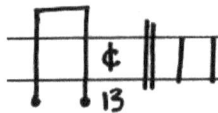

"TAIL" LOC

ADDITIONAL BODY LOCATIONS

Additional locations can be created as needed for precise locations on the body.

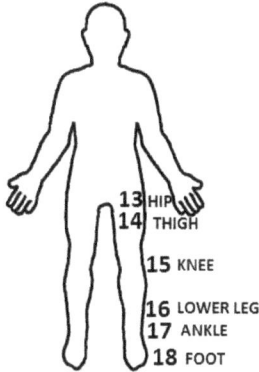

13 HIP
14 THIGH
15 KNEE
16 LOWER LEG
17 ANKLE
18 FOOT

THE ARM AND HAND

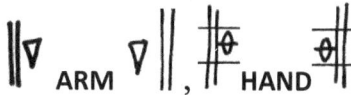

ARM , HAND

The arm and hands are composed of joints and bones. Starting at the shoulder, each **joint** is labeled alphabetically in uppercase: **A, B, C.** Beginning with the upper arm, each **bone** segment is labeled numerically: **1, 2.**

SHOULDER **A**
UPPER ARM **1**
C WRIST
2 FOREARM
B ELBOW

SAMPLE SIGN LOCATIONS: ARM

"RESPONSIBLE" LOC

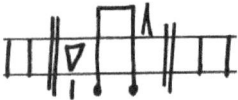

"BLOOD PRESSURE" LOC

"TEMPTATION" LOC

"DOCTOR" LOC
"PHYSICIAN"

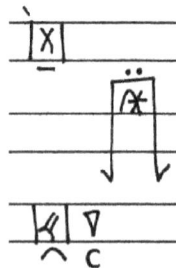

"TIME"

(A BASE HANDSHAPE SIGN)

HAND AND FINGER IDENTIFICATION

The fingers are numbered **1-5.** Each of the three finger joints are labeled alphabetically lowercase: **a, b, c.** Each of the 3 finger bones are labeled numerically: **.1, .2, .3.** The palm is "**0**", and the fingernail = **#.** This allows the specific location on the finger to be accurately notated as needed.

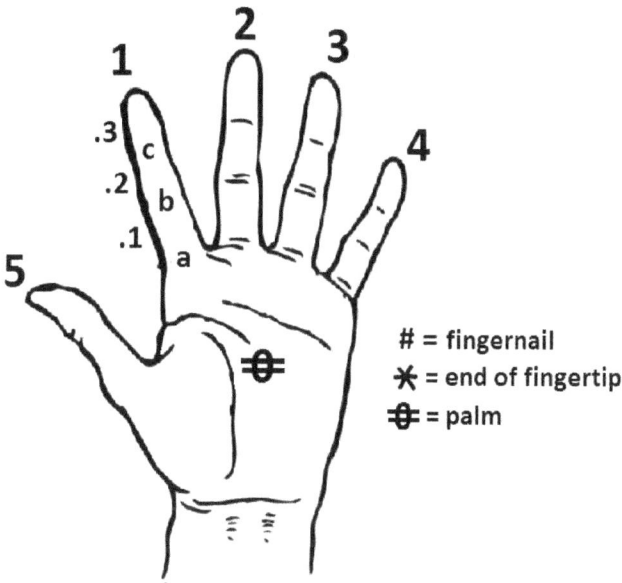

= fingernail
✳ = end of fingertip
✺ = palm

When recording on the SS staff, the ARM, HAND and FINGER locations critical for clear articulation will be listed **above** the applicable **HS block.**

FINGER LOCATION

THUMB

"SECRET"
"PRIVATE"
"PASS" (WORD)
"CLANDESTINE"
"CONFIDENTIAL"

A specific finger can also be indicated by using the finger number (1-5) circled either in the movement block or above or below the handshape. In the examples below the index or #1 finger is circled:

Example #1:

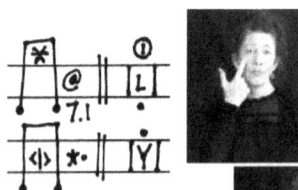

"LOOK LIKE"
"RESEMBLE"
"SIMILAR"

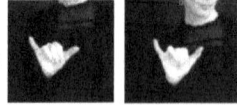

Example #2:

"LOOK LIKE"
"RESEMBLE"
"SIMILAR"

THE PALM

NON DOMINANT   **DOMINANT**

TOP SURFACE OF THE PALM IE: "WARRANT"

"WARRANT"

NOTE: FOR A BHSP, THE PALM CROSS SECTION IS THE
DEFAULT LOCATION FOR CONTACT

INSIDE EDGE OF ND PALM   IE: "MEAT"

"MEAT"
"CONTENT" (SUBJECT)

THE FOUR FACES OF THE ARM

The four faces of the wrist and other arm locations use simple dots around the exterior of the location. Here are the four faces of the wrist:

"DUTY" LOC

"DOCTOR" LOC

"CYST ON WRIST" (INSIDE)

"CYST ON WRIST" (OUTSIDE)

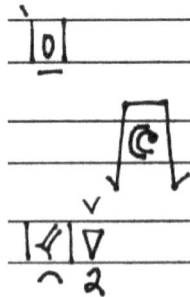

"HANDCUFF" LOC

"X-RAY: WRIST"

PARAMETER #4
MOVEMENT
LINES AND WHEELS

(P4) ASL MOVEMENTS CHART

DM:1 UP — NORTH, TALL, ROCKET LIFT-OFF	**DM:2** DOWN — SOUTH, THIRSTY, SNOW	**DM:3** RIGHT — EAST/WEST, PERSON WALKS R	**DM:4** LEFT — EAST/WEST, PERSON WALKS L	**DM:5** AWAY FROM SIGNER — I GIVE-YOU, DRIVE STRAIGHT AHEAD
DM:6 TOWARDS SIGNER — YOU-PAY-ME, PERSON APPROACHES ME	**DM:7** AWAY FROM SIGNER (L) — EVICT/DEPORT (L)	**DM:8** AWAY FROM SIGNER (R) — COMMUTE TO WORK (R)	**DM:9** TOWARDS SIGNER (L) — SHE-HELPS-ME (FROM L)	**DM:10** TOWARDS SIGNER (R) — HE-EMAILS-ME (FROM R)
DM:11 DIAGONAL: UP + LEFT — ROCKET DIAGONAL L	**DM:12** DIAGONAL: UP + RIGHT — ROCKET DIAGONAL R	**DM:13** DIAGONAL: DOWN + LEFT — UGLY (L HAND)	**DM:14** DIAGONAL: DOWN + RIGHT — UGLY (R HAND)	**DM:19** SIDE TO SIDE HORIZONTALLY — TRAVEL TO AND FRO
DM:20 UP AND DOWN VERTICALLY — ELEVATOR	**DM:18** UPWARD ANGLE — LEARN	**DM:17** DOWNWARD ANGLE — KNOCKED OUT, UNCONSCIOUS	**DM:16** DOWNWARD WITH FORCE — BANKRUPT	**FM:1** WIGGLE — COLOR, SNOW
FM:2 FLICK — TOO BAD, HATE, FEEDBACK	**FM:3** SCISSOR — SHEEP, HAIRCUT	**FM:4** SNAP — DOG	**FM:5** PINCH — MEAT, SKIN	**FM:6** WALK — WALK AROUND
FM:7 CLIMB — WALK UPSTAIRS/DOWNSTAIRS	**FM:8** KNUCKLE BOB — MOUSE, RABBIT	**FM:9** FINGER BOB 1X — SNAP A PHOTO	**FM:10** SIDE BOB — "NO-NO" GESTURE	**FM:11** QUESTION MARK — GOVERNMENT, ASK A QUESTION (?)
FM:12 SQUEEZE IN PLACE REPEATEDLY — MAD, SPONGE, WANT, INSECT	**M:1** HOP — DOLPHIN, CHILDREN, HARD OF HEARING	**M:2** VIBRATE — FISH, PLAY, FOR-FOR?, MEDICINE, WHERE, MOVIE, SILLY, FINISH, BLUE	**M:3** BOUNCE — HAT, CHILD	**M:4** WRIST NOD — YES, HAVE TO
M:5 CLOCKWISE CIRCLE — MONDAY, GESTURE	**M:6** COUNTER CLOCKWISE CIRCLE — SIGNING, ASIA, PLEASE	**M:7** FULL CIRCLE OUTWARD — FAMILY	**M:8** FULL CIRCLE INWARD — PLACE, AREA	**M:9** ARCS UPWARD — GO/COME, RAINBOW
M:10 ARCS DOWNWARD — ELEPHANT, WELCOME	**M:11** BACK AND FORTH, SIDE TO SIDE — WHAT, ANIMAL, TRAIN, ELEVATOR	**M:12** HS GOES THRU HS — GREY, EMAIL	**M:13** HS GOES UNDER HS — SNEAK OUT, KICK, HIDE	**M:14** HS ON TOP OF HS — CHAMP!, PUT ON A CHARACTER

POKE M:15	TWIST M:16	THROW M:17	REVERSE THROW M:18	WRIST FLIP M:19
OWE S, TAP FOR ATTENTION	KEY, COOL/NEAT, VOICE OFF	ASL, THROW OUT/GARBAGE	AND, COPY, LEARN, CATCH A BALL	COOK, DIE

WRIST FLIP + ROLL M:20	WRIST FLIP FIRM 1X M:21	WRIST ROCK SIDE-TO-SIDE M:22	HS OPENS AND CLOSES M:23	ARCS M:24
HOW, HAPPEN	BLUE (FIRM), FINISH	GREEN, ARGUE, CHUBBY, DANCE, WOW	MILK, BIRD, NO	CAR, TRUCK, PARIS

SHAKE M:25	SCOOP AND LIFT M:26	SOFT "?" M:27	PARTIAL CIRCLE M:28	SWIRL M:29
BATHROOM, WHERE, SIMILAR, BAR	NEW, WHAT'S UP?	NEVER, FUN, CHICAGO	IMPORTANT	BEAUTIFUL, AFRICA, X-RAY

CONTACT CM:1	TAPPING CM:2	FINGERTIP CONTACT CM:3	GLANCE OFF CM:4	INTERTWINE CLASP CM:5
SCHOOL, GAME	WARN, CRACKER, DENTIST	BIRTHDAY, EQUAL	PAPER, CLEAN, STAR	MARRIED HAMBURGER, FRIEND

FINGERS INTERSECT CM:6	FINGERS INTERSECT AT BASE CM:7	TAPPING FINGERTIP CM:8	FINGERS OVERLAP CM:9	FINGERTIP GLANCE OFF CM:10
AMERICA	PREGNANT, FOOTBALL	FAVORITE, MAMA, MORE	NAME	I-PAD, CAT

HINGE CM:11	CROSSED ARMS CM:12	FIRM CONTACT CM:13	CONTACT + BOUNCE CM:14	FIRM CONTACT + BOUNCE CM:15
BOOK, PURSE	BEAR, LOVE, REST, SECURE	RIGHT, ESTABLISH	ON-TIME, PRINT	ILLEGAL, TRICK/TOOL

TAP-TAP (2) FINGERTIP FIRM CM:16	PARALLEL CM:17	APPROACHES WITHOUT CONTACT CM:18	KISS CM:19	SCRATCH CM:20
OWE S	PARALLEL, HIGHWAY	REDUCE, MEET SOMEONE, NEAR	KISS-FIST	BEAR, ANALYZE, SUSPECT

CONTACT CONTINUOUS CM:21	PINCH-PULL CM:22	PULL APART CM:23	DRAGS CM:24	CONTACT, BOUNCE, CONTACT CM:25
ROMANCE, EMPHASIZE	VOLUNTEER, HAIR	STORY, SENTENCE	HUNGRY, DEPRESSED, CRY	BIRTHDAY, LESSON, DEAF, HOME, PARENTS

WAVE+DRAGS CM:26	CRADLE ARMS CM:27	CONTACT + UP-SWOOP CM:28	TWIST + TURN FORWARD CM:29	TOUCH, TURN, TOUCH CM:30
DRAW PICTURE, METH	DAUGHTER/SON, BABY	COLLEGE, UNIVERSITY	CRAFTS, TO MAKE	TO MAKE

ROTATE, TOUCH CM:31	(BOTH HANDS) CM:32	(BOTH HANDS) CM:33	(BOTH HANDS) CM:34
COOKIE, BUDGET	HOUSE, CAMP, TENT	CAMPING	SYSTEM, ALTAR

(P4) CLOSE UP

DM = DIRECTIONAL MOVEMENT
FM = FINGER MOVEMENT
M = MOVEMENT
CM = CONTACT MOVEMENT

DM = DIRECTIONAL MOVEMENT

3-D directional movement notations can stand alone as a direction for a sign movement, or in conjunction with another sign movement that requires a directional component.

Note: All of the following are samples of possible movement notations. They are experimental and can be re-designed by the Deaf Community to fit any particular, unique sign language movement. Each movement must be connected to an actual sign in use. **Some movements require the addition of a direction, and some require more than one movement notation.** See: "embedded movements" in the Grammar Section that follows, (ie: hurricane).

Movements are from the signer's perspective or from the right side.

DIMENSION #1 ⯲ VERTICAL

UP DM:1	DOWN DM:2
NORTH, TALL, ROCKET LIFT-OFF	SOUTH, THIRSTY, SNOW

DIMENSION #2 ✝ LATERAL

| RIGHT | DM:3 |
| EAST/WEST, PERSON WALKS R |

| LEFT | DM:4 |
| EAST/WEST, PERSON WALKS L |

DIMENSION #3 ⊤ HORIZONTAL

| AWAY FROM SIGNER | DM:5 |
| I-GIVE-YOU, DRIVE STRAIGHT AHEAD |

| TOWARDS SIGNER | DM:6 |
| YOU-PAY-ME PERSON APPROACHES ME |

| AWAY FROM SIGNER (L) | DM:7 |
| EVICT/DEPORT (L) |

| AWAY FROM SIGNER (R) | DM:8 |
| COMMUTE TO WORK (R) |

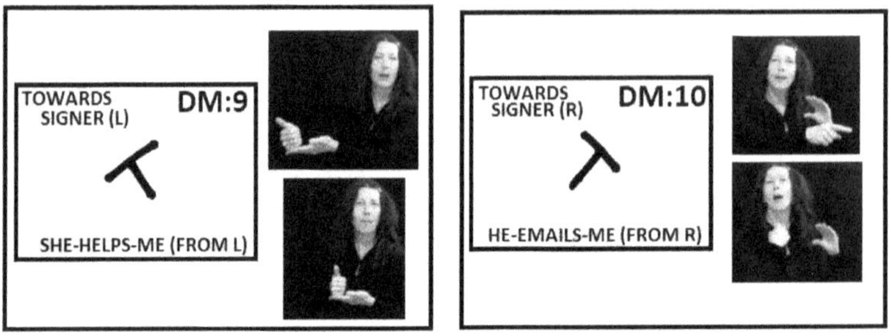

DIMENSIONS #1 & 2

VERTICAL LATERAL

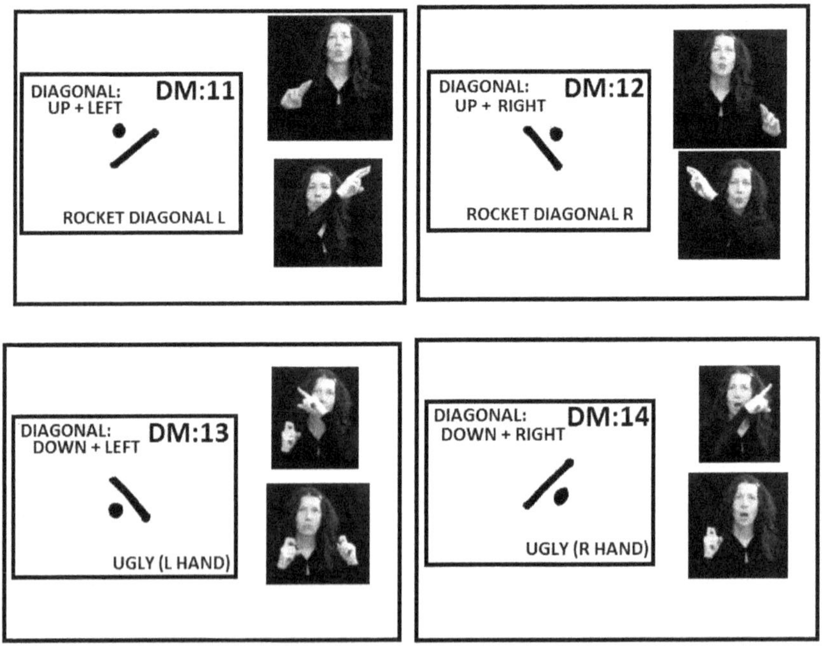

SIDE TO SIDE **DM:19**
HORIZONTALLY

TRAVEL TO AND FRO

UP AND DOWN **DM:20**
VERTICALLY

ELEVATOR

*TO ANGLE DIMENSION #3 UPWARD, ADD 1 DOT

UPWARD **DM: 18**
ANGLE

LEARN

*TO ANGLE DIMENSION #3 DOWNWARD, ADD 2 DOTS

DOWNWARD **DM:17**
ANGLE

KNOCKED OUT,
UNCONSCIOUS

ADDING FORCE TO ANY DIRECTIONAL MOVEMENTS:

UPWARD WITH FORCE **DM:15**

STROKE, RAISE HEAVY WINDOW

DOWNWARD WITH FORCE **DM:16**

BANKRUPT

FM = FINGER MOVEMENT

WIGGLE **FM:1**

COLOR, SNOW

FLICK **FM:2**

TOO BAD, HATE, FEEDBACK

SCISSOR **FM:3**

SHEEP, HAIRCUT

SNAP **FM:4**

DOG

PINCH | FM:5

S

MEAT, SKIN

WALK | FM:6

WALK AROUND

CLIMB | FM:7

WALK UPSTAIRS/DOWNSTAIRS

KNUCKLE BOB | FM:8

MOUSE, RABBIT

FINGER BOB 1X | FM:9

SNAP A PHOTO

SIDE BOB | FM:10

"NO-NO" GESTURE

QUESTION MARK | FM:11

?

GOVERNMENT, ASK A QUESTION QQ

SQUEEZE IN PLACE REPEATEDLY | FM: 12

MAD, SPONGE, WANT, INSECT

M = MOVEMENT

M:1 HOP — DOLPHIN, CHILDREN, HARD OF HEARING

M:2 VIBRATE — FISH, PLAY, FOR-FOR?, BLUE, SILLY, FINISH, MEDICINE, WHERE, MOVIE

M:3 BOUNCE — HAT, CHILD

M:4 WRIST NOD — YES, HAVE TO

M:5 CLOCKWISE CIRCLE — MONDAY, GESTURE

M:6 COUNTER-CLOCKWISE CIRCLE — SIGNING, ASIA, PLEASE

M:7 FULL CIRCLE OUTWARD — FAMILY

M:8 FULL CIRCLE INWARD — PLACE, AREA

ARCS UPWARD M:9

GO/COME, RAINBOW

ARCS DOWNWARD M:10

ELEPHANT, WELCOME

BACK AND FORTH, SIDE TO SIDE M:11

WHAT, ANIMAL, TRAIN, ELEVATOR

HS GOES THRU HS M:12

GREY, EMAIL

HS GOES UNDER HS M:13

SNEAK OUT, KICK, HIDE

HS ON TOP OF HS M:14

CHAMP!
PUT ON A CHARACTER

POKE M:15

OWE $,
TAP FOR ATTENTION

TWIST M:16

KEY, COOL/NEAT,
VOICE OFF

THROW **M:17**

ASL,
THROW OUT/GARBAGE

REVERSE THROW **M:18**

AND, COPY,
LEARN, CATCH A BALL

WRIST FLIP **M:19**

COOK, DIE

WRIST FLIP + ROLL **M:20**

HOW, HAPPEN

WRIST FLIP FIRM **M: 21**
1X

BLUE (FIRM), FINISH

WRIST ROCK **M: 22**
SIDE-TO-SIDE

GREEN, ARGUE,
CHUBBY, DANCE, WOW

HS OPENS **M: 23**
AND CLOSES

MILK, BIRD, NO

ARCS **M: 24**

OR

CAR, TRUCK, PARIS

SHAKE **M: 25**

BATHROOM, WHERE, SIMILAR, BAR

SCOOP AND LIFT **M: 26**

NEW, WHAT'S UP?

SOFT "7" **M: 27**

NEVER, FUN, CHICAGO

PARTIAL CIRCLE **M: 28**

IMPORTANT

SWIRL **M:29**

OR

BEAUTIFUL, AFRICA, X-RAY

CM = CONTACT MOVEMENT

CONTACT **CM:1**

SCHOOL, GAME

TAPPING **CM:2**

WARN, CRACKER, DENTIST

FINGERTIP CONTACT — CM:3
BIRTHDAY, EQUAL

TAPPING FINGERTIP — CM:8
FAVORITE, MAMA, MORE

GLANCE OFF — CM:4
PAPER, CLEAN, STAR

INTERTWINE CLASP — CM:5
MARRIED HAMBURGER, FRIEND

FINGERS INTERSECT — CM:6
AMERICA

FINGERS INTERSECT AT BASE — CM:7
PREGNANT, FOOTBALL

FINGERS OVERLAP — CM:9
NAME

FINGERTIP GLANCE-OFF — CM:10
I-PAD, CAT

HINGE	**CM:11**
	⋈
	BOOK, PURSE

CROSSED ARMS	**CM: 12**
	XX
	BEAR, LOVE, REST, SECURE

FIRM CONTACT	**CM:13**
	X̄W
	RIGHT, ESTABLISH

CONTACT + BOUNCE	**CM:14**
	Ẋ
	ON-TIME, PRINT

FIRM CONTACT + BOUNCE	**CM:15**
	ẇ
	ILLEGAL, TRICK/FOOL

TAP-TAP (2) FINGERTIP FIRM	**CM:16**
	⋉W
	OWE $

PARALLEL	**CM:17**
	‖
	PARALLEL, HIGHWAY

APPROACHES WITHOUT CONTACT	**CM:18**
	|x
	REDUCE MEET SOMEONE, NEAR

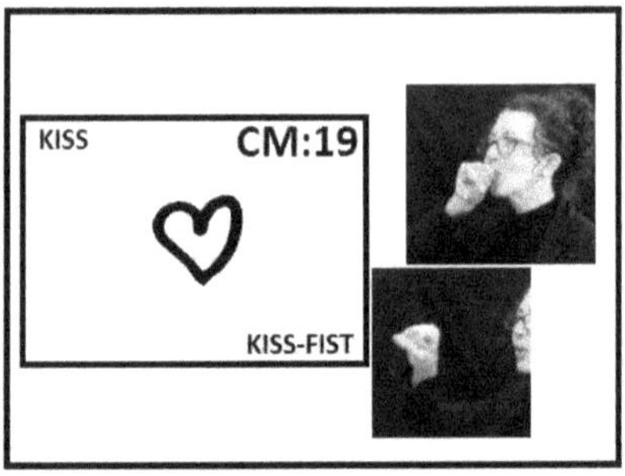
KISS
CM:19
KISS-FIST

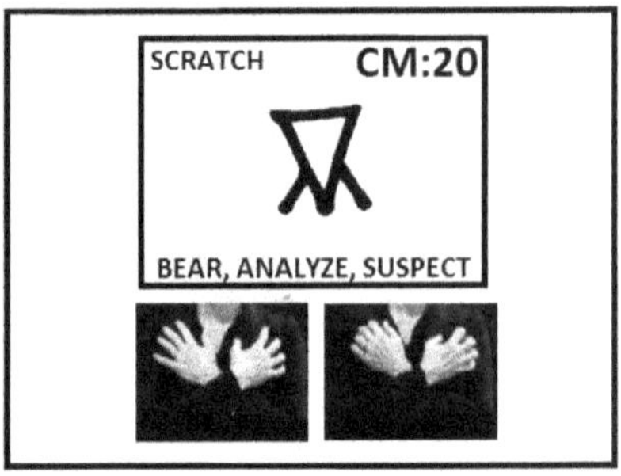
SCRATCH
CM:20
BEAR, ANALYZE, SUSPECT

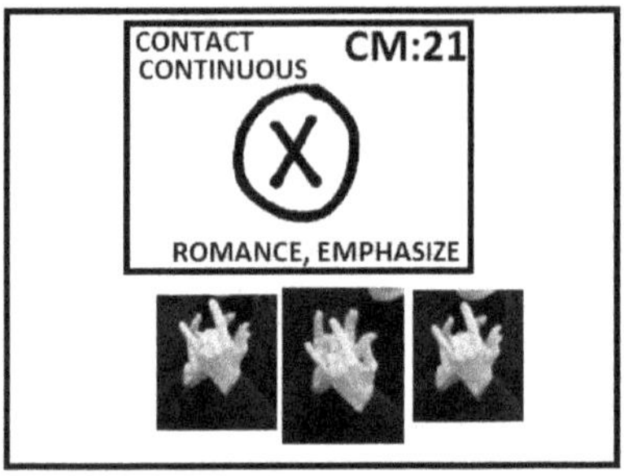
CONTACT CONTINUOUS
CM:21
ROMANCE, EMPHASIZE

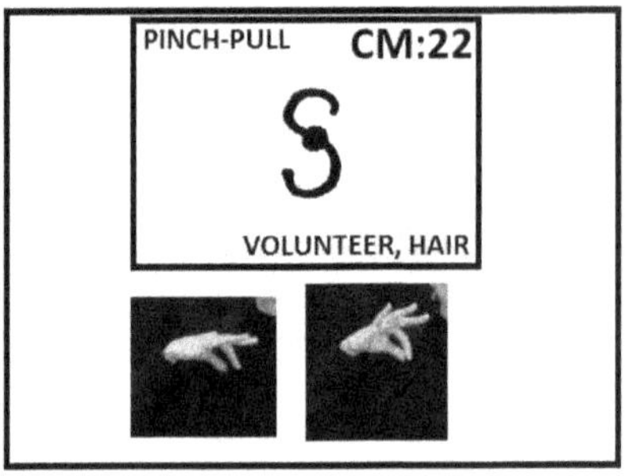
PINCH-PULL
CM:22
VOLUNTEER, HAIR

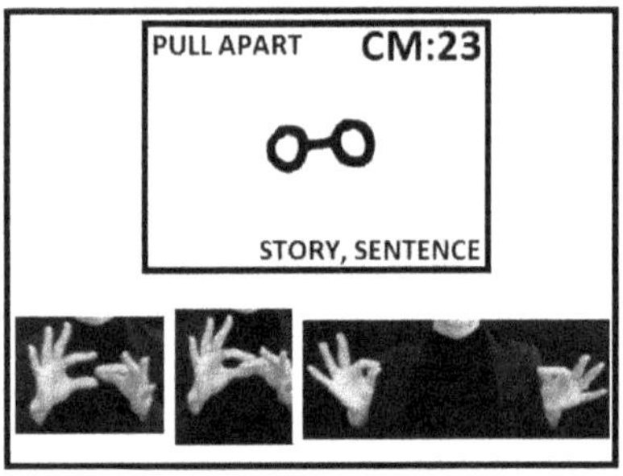
PULL APART
CM:23
STORY, SENTENCE

DRAGS
CM:24
HUNGRY, DEPRESSED, CRY

CONTACT, BOUNCE, CONTACT
CM:25
BIRTHDAY, LESSON, DEAF, HOME, PARENTS

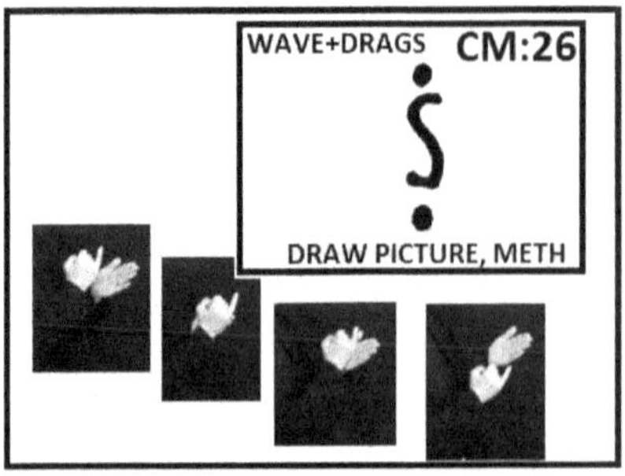
WAVE+DRAGS
CM:26
DRAW PICTURE, METH

CRADLE ARMS **CM: 27**

DAUGHTER/SON, BABY

CONTACT + UP-SWOOP **CM: 28**

COLLEGE, UNIVERSITY

TWIST + TURN **CM: 29**
FORWARD

CRAFTS, TO MAKE

TOUCH, TURN, **CM: 30**
TOUCH

TO MAKE

TOUCH, **CM: 31**
ROTATE,
TOUCH

COOKIE, BUDGET

(BOTH HANDS) **CM: 32**

HOUSE, CAMP, TENT

(BOTH HANDS) **CM: 33**

CAMPING

(BOTH HANDS) **CM: 34**

SYSTEM, ALTAR

S. HANSEN

REPETITION IN MVT OR CONTACT

REPEATED MVTS

Dots above the MVT block notate the number of reps:

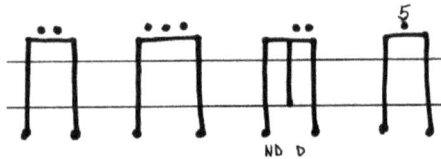

NĐ Ð

Many signs have only one MVT or Contact and do not need any rep dots, as default is one single movement. In ASL, nouns commonly have two smaller reps and verbs have one stronger rep. The ND and D HS rep sections can be notated separately, and a number used with a rep dot for multiple-rep MVTS. The general rule is to use rep dots for 1-3 MVT reps and a single dot with the total number of reps written as a number for 4 or more reps.

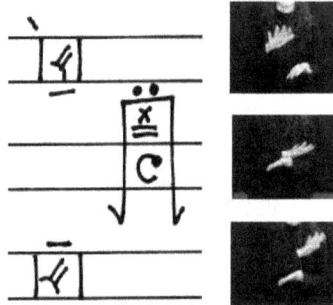

"PAPER"

ODD NUMBER OF REPS

Some signs include contact and an odd number of reps. For example the sign "cook" can have three contacts and two movements and can be notated as a fraction:

96

"COOK"

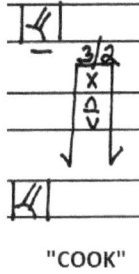

NUMBER HS REPETITIONS

"to
print"   "newspaper"
"understand"

When using numbers that have a movement as a HS, identify the number of reps within the HS block.

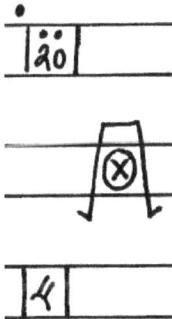

"NEWSPAPER"

ALTERNATE NOTATION FOR SERIAL MOVEMENTS

Signs with the same handshape and same movement but different locations can be notated using a comma between locations, for example:

"RESTAURANT"

LOCKED-HANDSHAPE MVTS

or

Some signs have one moving handshape (usually the dominant HS), and one "locked" handshape. For example:

"EXPIRED"

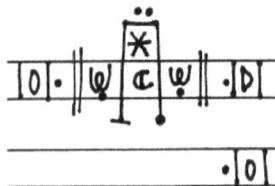

"ONE MORE"

98

"INTERPRETER"

FINGERTIP CONTACT MOVEMENTS

To notate a specific fingertip, write the number of the finger (1 ,2, 3, 4 or 5) circled in the contact section of the movement block. Default contact is at the point of greatest extension.

"FLIRT"

CHANGES IN MOVEMENT SIZE

Many sign meanings are modified by the size and speed of a root sign. These changes are similar to changes in tempo and time signature in music, but have semantic implications in signed languages, and can be notated.

LARGE MOVEMENT   SMALL MOVEMENT

MOVEMENT SPEED

1-2

4-5

SLOW MOVEMENTS (1 OR 2)   FAST MOVEMENTS (4 0R 5)
3 = AVERAGE SPEED

Note: Default is small rapid movements and large slower movements, therefore the number notation is optional.

EXAMPLES OF MOVEMENT
SIZE AND SPEED NOTATION:

"DAILY"
"EVERYDAY"
"REGULARLY"

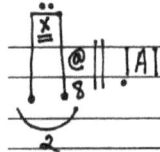

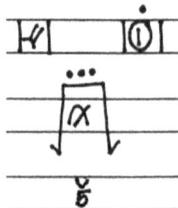

"DAILY"
"EVERYDAY"
"REGULARLY"

"ALARM
OR
PHONE RINGING"

CIRCULAR MOVEMENTS: DIRECTIONALITY

Circular movements require directionality notation to know which plane is being used. The three planes can be notated below the circular movement. Default is the vertical plane such as the sign "PLEASE".

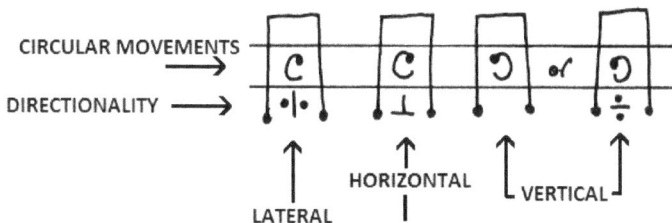

VERTICAL

"COMPUTER"

"PLEASE"

LATERAL

"HERE"

"WASH THE TABLE"

HORIZONTAL

"DRAMA"

also: "ASL"

"AGGRESSIVE"

S. HANSEN

PARAMETER #5
FACIAL GRAMMAR

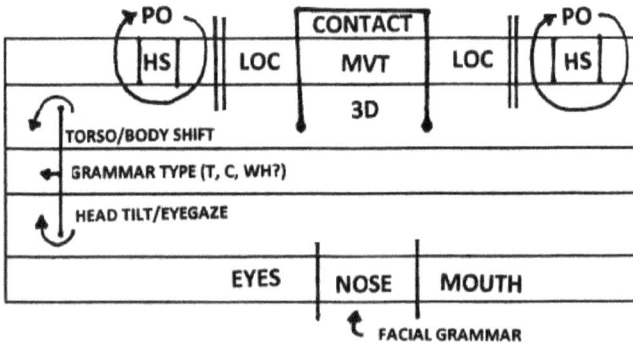

			CONTACT			
PO HS		LOC	MVT	LOC		PO HS
			3D			

TORSO/BODY SHIFT

GRAMMAR TYPE (T, C, WH?)

HEAD TILT/EYEGAZE

	EYES	NOSE	MOUTH

FACIAL GRAMMAR

(P5) TYPE 1: FACIAL GRAMMAR CHART

GRAMMAR BOX

T	C	WH	Y/N	RH	3

(P5) TYPE 2: FACIAL MORPHEMES CHART

EYES

SQUINTY EYES FGe: 1	FURROWED BROWS FGe: 2	WIDE OPEN EYES FGe: 3	EYES TRACK SIGN (SPOTLIGHT) FGe: 4	RAPID EYE BLINKING FGe: 5
SMALL AMOUNT, TINY	ANGRY, MAD, UPSET	THIS, OR THAT? (COMPARISON)	LOOK ON PAGE 36	BE UNAWARE OF, SERIOUSLY? THAT'S UNUSUAL...

UPWARD GAZE FGe: 6	DOWNWARD GAZE FGe: 7	EYES CLOSED FGe: 8	EYES ROLL FGe: 9	EYE BROWS RAISED FGe: 10
REMEMBERING, THINKING	LOOK FOR SOMETHING, GUILTY, SUBMISSIVE	IGNORING, NOT LISTENING	ANNOYANCE, OH BROTHER	Y/N QUESTIONS, PAY ATTENTION

NOSE

NOSE WRINKLE: REPEATING (X2) FGn: 1	NOSE WRINKLE: HELD FGn: 2
YES, AFFIRMATIVE	HUH? WHAT?

MOUTH

OOOoo **FGm: 1** OO	CHA **FGm: 2** CHA	PAH! **FGm: 3** PAH	BING **FGm: 4** BING	ONE CHEEK PUFF **FGm: 5** -O
LONG TIME AGO, LITTLE BIT, SMALL	LARGE AMT, BIG	FINALLY! SUCCESS!	TEND TO, TYPICALLY	CYST, LUMP

PUFFED CHEEKS **FGm: 6** O—O	FSH **FGm: 7**	MMM **FGm: 8** mm	LOWER LIP IN AND OUT **FGm: 9** OIC	KISS **FGm: 10** ♡
FAT, CHUBBY	FINISH, DONE, STOP IT	(DRIVING AVE SPEED) MED SIZE, AVERAGE	THAT'S INTERESTING... OH, I SEE...	KISS-FIST, LOVE IT! FAV

LOWER TEETH EXPOSED **FGm: 11**	TONGUE HALF-OUT **FGm: 12**	BLOWING AIR **FGm: 13**)C	OPEN MOUTH **FGm: 14** θ	TEETH EXPOSED **FGm: 15**	SCHA-JAH **FGm: 16**
ACCIDENTALLY RUINED, MISTAKE	NOT-YET, AWKWARD, CLUMSY	NOTHING, WINDY	SHOCK, OBSESS OVER	BRUSH TEETH	SPEECH, SPEECH PRACTICE

RASPBERRY LIPS/BUZZ **FGm: 17** B	BOW/POW **FGm: 18** OW	SMILE **FGM: 19**	FROWN **FGm: 20**	TONGUE SWALLOW **FGm: 21**	SHU-ZSHA **FGm: 22** ΠU
BORED, OH BROTHER	SHUT DOWN, BOMB BLAST	BE HAPPY, SAY CHEESE	BE SAD, UNHAPPY	ALL GONE, DISAPPEAR, GULLIBLE	MAKE FUN OF, TEASE

PTH **FGm: 23**	HALF CHEEK PULL **FGm: 24** 7	BOTH LIPS PUFFY **FGm: 25** ∞	JAW DROP **FGm: 26** U	TONGUE SIDE TO SIDE, RAPIDLY **FGm: 27**	COVER MOUTH **FGm: 28**
MELT AWAY, DECOMPOSE	RECENTLY	COMFORTABLE, MAKE A DECISION	STUNNED, SHOCKED	WANT, HAVE TO/MUST, AWESOME, COOL	NAUSEOUS, MISTAKE/OOPS

P5 TYPE 1: SENTENCE TYPE

GRAMMAR BOX

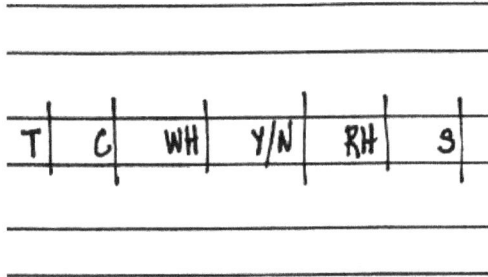

The first type of notation for facial grammar can be recorded in the GRAMMAR BOX (ie: Topic/Comment, WH?, Y/N?, RH?, Statement etc...) This enables the signer to know the prescribed facial grammar needed for the upcoming section. For example, here are some common WH ? signs:

"What?" "Where?" "Why?" "Which?" "For-for?"

Below is a simple WH? sentence that includes grammatically prescribed facial expression:

"How many children?" "Five."

Here is that same WH question in signotation:

Below is a simple Yes/No? sentence that includes grammatically prescribed facial expression:

"Want   milk"   "Yes, No?"

Here is that same Y/N question in signotation:

Here is a simple Topic/Comment sentence that includes grammatically prescribed facial expression:

Topic

Comment

T: "My   car...   C: blue."

Here is that same Topic/Comment statement in signotation:

There are other grammatical constructions, such as conditional statements and imperatives, as well as three more important grammatical features that can be recorded in the Grammar Block: **Torso/Role shifting, Head tilt** and **Eye gaze**.

107

TORSO SHIFT

Position ✿
center
"narrator"

Position 1
torso shift (R)

Position 2
torso shift (L)

HEAD TILT & EYE GAZE

Upward
gaze

Center
gaze

Downward
gaze

Upward
gaze
Position
1

Upward
gaze
Position
2

Downward
gaze
Position
1

Downward
gaze
Position
2

P5 TYPE 2: FACIAL MORPHEMES

EYES, NOSE, MOUTH

Specific facial grammar is recorded left to right: EYE, NOSE, MOUTH on the third tier of the signing staff, below the movement block:

SAMPLE: FACIAL GRAMAR TYPE 2:

FACIAL GRAMMAR TYPE 2:

EYES TRACK SIGN (SPOTLIGHT)

FGe: 4

LOOK ON PAGE 36

EYES NOSE MOUTH

"MIRROR"

NOTE: The notations listed in this section are for illustrative purposes to show how various aspects of facial grammar can be identified, connected to a concrete sign or meaning, and recorded. The symbols themselves are arbitrary, and can be modified or replaced by the Deaf Community. Alternative facial grammar expressions can be added or removed by any community of sign language users to record the 5th parameter.

EYES

FGe = FACIAL GRAMMAR eyes

SQUINTY EYES FGe: 1	FURROWED BROWS FGe: 2	WIDE OPEN EYES FGe: 3
SMALL AMOUNT, TINY	ANGRY, MAD, UPSET	THIS, OR THAT? (COMPARISON)

EYES TRACK SIGN (SPOTLIGHT)	FGe: 4

LOOK ON PAGE 36

RAPID EYE BLINKING	FGe: 5

BE UNAWARE OF, SERIOUSLY?
THAT'S UNUSUAL...

UPWARD GAZE	FGe: 6

REMEMBERING, THINKING

DOWNWARD GAZE	FGe: 7

LOOK FOR SOMETHING, GUILTY, SUBMISSIVE

EYES CLOSED	FGe: 8

IGNORING, NOT LISTENING

EYES ROLL	FGe: 9

ANNOYANCE, OH BROTHER

EYE BROWS RAISED	FGe: 10

Y/N QUESTIONS, PAY ATTENTION

NOSE

FGn = FACIAL GRAMMAR nose

MOUTH

FGm = FACIAL GRAMMAR mouth

OOOoo **FGm: 1** OO	CHA **FGm: 2** CHA	PAH! **FGm: 3** PAH
LONG TIME AGO, LITTLE BIT, SMALL	LARGE AMT, BIG	FINALLY! SUCCESS!
BING **FGm: 4** BING	ONE CHEEK PUFF **FGm: 5**	PUFFED CHEEKS **FGm: 6**
TEND TO, TYPICALLY	CYST, LUMP	FAT, CHUBBY

FSH | FGm: 7
FINISH, DONE, STOP IT

MMM | FGm: 8 mm
(DRIVING AVE SPEED)
MED SIZE, AVERAGE

LOWER LIP IN AND OUT | FGm: 9
OIC
THAT'S INTERESTING...
OH, I SEE...

KISS | FGm: 10
KISS-FIST, LOVE IT! FAV

LOWER TEETH EXPOSED | FGm: 11
ACCIDENTALLY
RUINED, MISTAKE

TONGUE HALF-OUT | FGm: 12
NOT-YET,
AWKWARD, CLUMSY

BLOWING AIR | FGm: 13
NOTHING, WINDY

OPEN MOUTH | FGm: 14
SHOCK, OBSESS OVER

TEETH EXPOSED | FGm: 15
BRUSH TEETH

114

SCHA-JAH **FGm: 16** SPEECH, SPEECH PRACTICE	RASPBERRY LIPS/BUZZ **FGm: 17** BORED, OH BROTHER	BOW/POW **FGm: 18** SHUT DOWN, BOMB BLAST
SMILE **FGM: 19** BE HAPPY, SAY CHEESE	FROWN **FGm: 20** BE SAD, UNHAPPY	TONGUE SWALLOW **FGm: 21** ALL GONE, DISAPPEAR, GULLIBLE
SHU-ZSHA **FGm: 22** MAKE FUN OF, TEASE	PTH **FGm: 23** MELT AWAY, DECOMPOSE	HALF CHEEK PULL **FGm: 24** RECENTLY

FGm: 25 — BOTH LIPS PUFFY — COMFORTABLE, MAKE A DECISION

FGm: 26 — JAW DROP — STUNNED, SHOCKED

FGm: 27 — TONGUE SIDE TO SIDE, RAPIDLY — WANT, HAVE TO/MUST, AWESOME, COOL

FGm: 28 — COVER MOUTH — NAUSEOUS, MISTAKE/OOPS

GRAMMAR NOTES

The following grammatical notes provide further guidance for accurately notating sign languages.

ALTERNATING MVTS

Many signs have an alternating movement pattern. The handshapes are the same, and the movements alternate from the dominant to non-dominant hand. Default location is Standard Signing Space unless otherwise notated, the number of repetitions is two (one full cycle) unless otherwise notated, and as both handshapes are the same, we can use an abbreviated format:

OR

Standard Signing Space

"ASL"

"CAR"
"AUTOMOBILE"

LATERAL ALTERNATING MOVEMENTS

(∞)

Some movements alternate laterally. An example is the sign glossed: "Jesus" which has an alternating pattern:

"JESUS"

NOTE: The palm location was added to clarify the ND contact location.

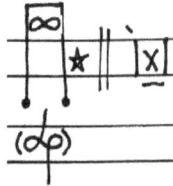

"FRIEND"

BASE HANDSHAPE PAIRS (BHS-P)

"COOKIE"

Because a Base Handshape is so common, we can create an iconic symbol for this HS. The standard BHS is an open "B" with the thumb extended out to the side, palm orientation upward to the sky and fingertips angled towards the midline, (ie: ND HS "cook"). Notated alone, the **default position** for the non-dominant BHS is palm up, fingertips angled to the midline in a relaxed position. The BHS-P location is in the **Standard Signing Space** unless otherwise notated. **Contact** is presumed **on the palm** area of a BHS unless otherwise notated.

NON DOMINANT BHS: Default Palm Orientation is up to the sky.

DOMINANT BHS
Palm Orientation must be notated.

BASE HANDSHAPE PAIRS: VERTICAL

A Vertical BHS serves as a foundation or support in the up and down or vertical plane. The majority of BHS-P are vertical.

V BHS FORMAT:

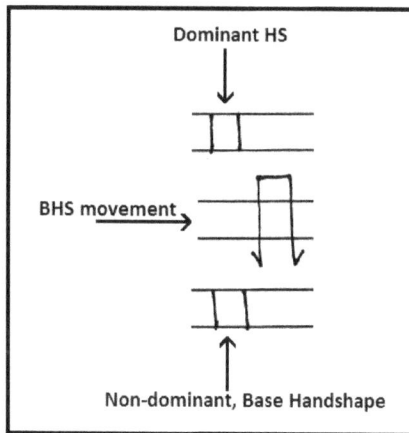

SAMPLE BASE HANDSHAPE PAIR: VERTICAL

"SCHOOL"

"NEW"

"TIME"

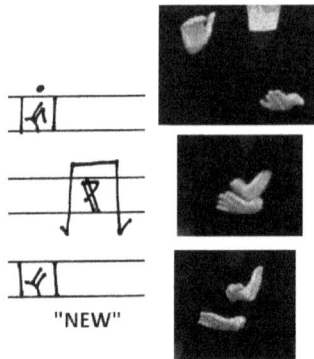

NOTE: The default location for the V BHS is the Standard Signing Space. The added wrist location for the sign "time", refers to a specific contact location on the BHS. Also note the BHS can vary as in this relaxed BHS for "time".

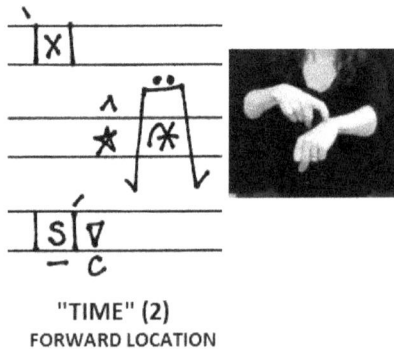

"TIME" (2)
FORWARD LOCATION

NOTE: A change in the overall location of the BHS-P can be notated to the left of the movement block, as in this sign which is articulated further forward in the signing space.

BASE HANDSHAPE PAIR VARIATIONS

A change in the relationship between the Dominant HS and Base Handshape can be notated mid-tier using the directional notations to indicate the D HS position:

D HS <u>below</u> the BHS:

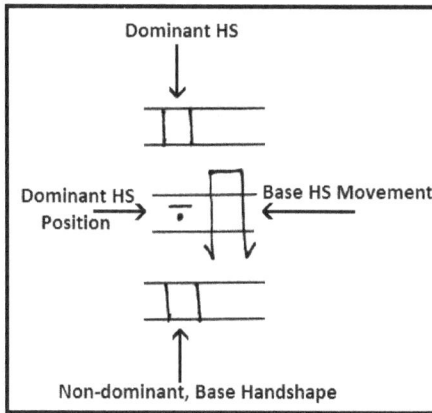

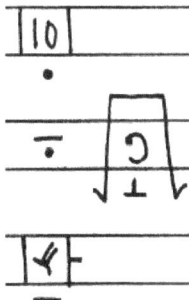

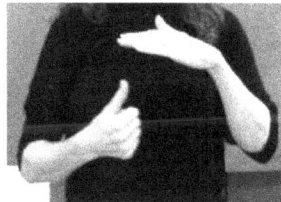

"BASEMENT"
"UNDERNEATH"

D HS <u>near</u> the signer's body:

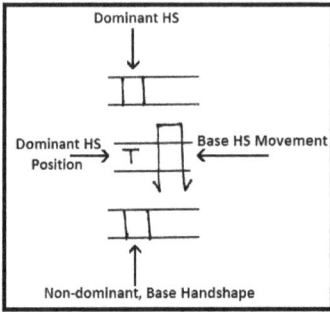

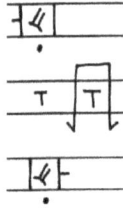

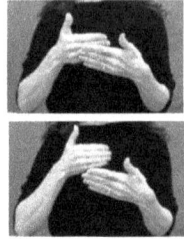

"BEFORE"
"PRIOR "
"AHEAD OF TIME"

HS <u>away from</u> the signer's body:

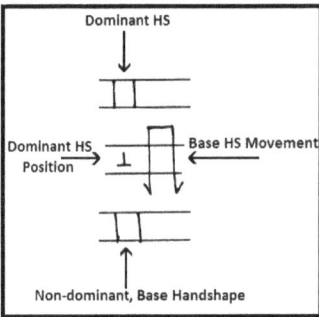

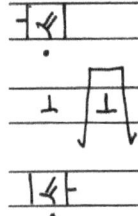

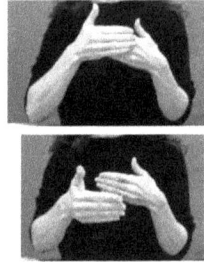

"AFTER"
"SUBSEQUENT"

D HS <u>mixed</u> position:

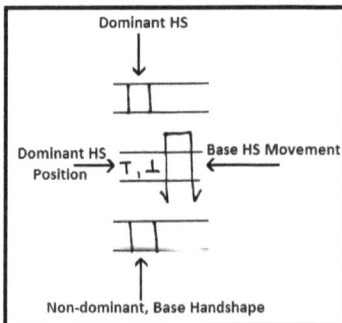

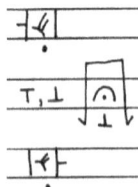

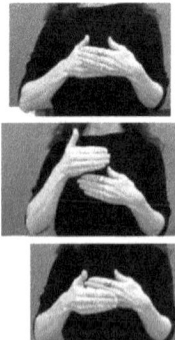

"NEXT"
"THEN"
"ADJACENT"

Base HANDSHAPE NUMERICAL
INCORPORATION

ASL has a complex system for numerical incorporation into standard signs. An example of a BHS-P is the numbering of months and these changes in number can be notated in the handshape block:

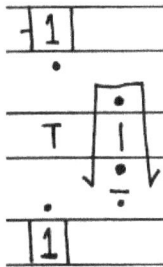

"ONE MONTH"

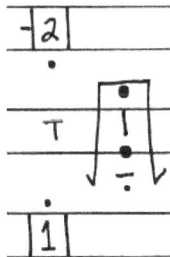

"TWO MONTHS"

"THREE MONTHS"   "FIVE MONTHS"

Base Handshape Pairs: Lateral

A lateral base handshape serves as a foundation or support In the side-to-side or horizontal plane.

L BHS FORMAT:

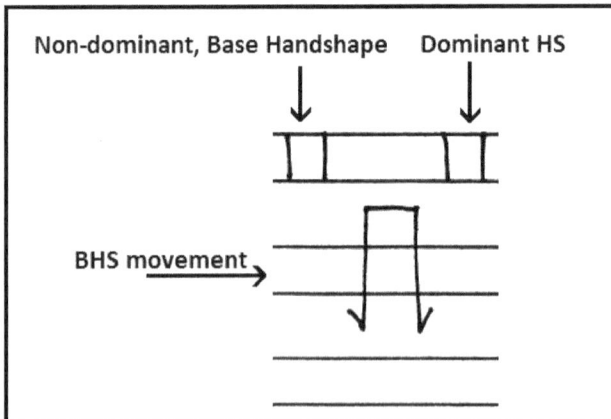

SAMPLE BASE HANDSHAPE: LATERAL

"ILLEGAL"
"PROHIBITED"
"UNLAWFUL"
"AGAINST THE RULES"

"FROM"

Alternative format for timelines:

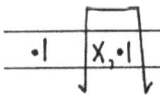

"BEFORE" (timeline)

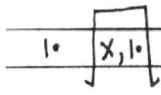

"AFTER" (timeline)

Palm Locations for BHSP

A notation to indicate whether a repeated BHSP movement occurs from the palm to fingertip area or fingertip to palm area is notated next to the movement block:

I>	>I
Palm to fingertip	Fingertip to palm

"OFTEN"

"LESSON"

Compound Signs

Some signs are created by joining two signs. In the example below, a one-handed sign: "SIGN" is combined with a BHS sign: "TO MAKE A NOTE" to form a new compound sign. A (>) symbol joins the two signs mid-staff:

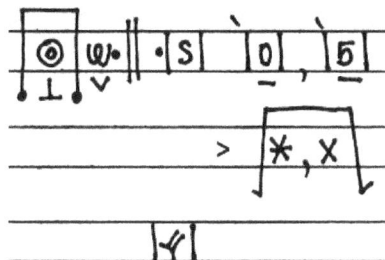

"SIGNOTATION"

Here are a few more examples:

"BABYSIT"
"CHILDCARE"

"GIRLFRIEND"

"HOMEWORK"
"ASSIGNMENT"

Conjugation of Verbs

ASL has a set of verbs that are conjugated in the same way romance languages (French, Spanish, Italian) conjugate verbs. Directional verbs in ASL take a root verb such as "teach" and conjugate or modify in consistent patterns to indicate first person, second person and third person. For example the verb "to teach" is modified directionally to express:

- I teach you
- You teach me
- I teach her/him/all of you
- You teach each other
- She teaches him

Here is a very brief list of a few sample verbs that are similarly conjugated in ASL:

- pay
- give

- call
- e-mail
- come
- go
- help

Not all directional verbs utilize all of the possible conjugated forms, but the basic pattern is consistent for these directionalized verbs.

STEP 1: IDENTIFY THE ROOT VERB

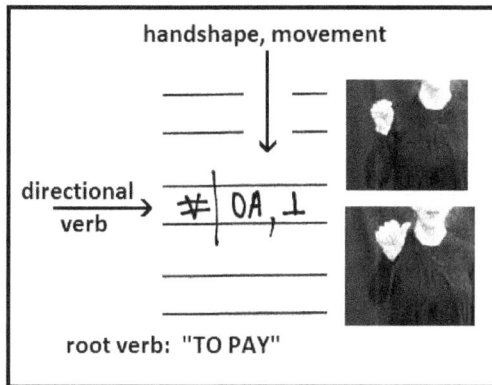

STEP 2: ADD THE CONJUGATED FORM USING DIRECTIONAL NOTATIONS

DIRECTIONALITY OF PRONOUNS

YOU	ME	HE, SHE, IT	HE, SHE, IT	YOU ALL	WE	THEY (R)	THEY (L)
⊥	T	Y	⋎	⏄	⏄	⍴	⍴

S. HANSEN

directional conjugate

⊥

‡ | O,A

"I pay you"

directional conjugate

T

‡ | O,A

"you pay me"

directional conjugate

Y

‡ | O,A

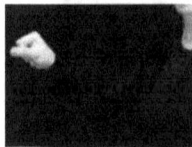

"I pay her/him" (right)

132

directional conjugate

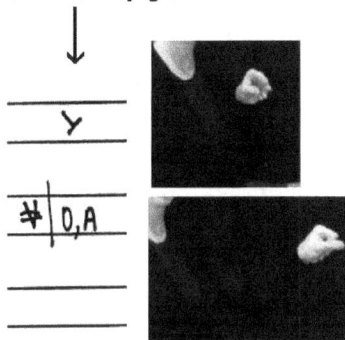

"I pay her/him" (left)

directional conjugate

"she/he pays me" (right)

directional conjugate

"she/he pays me" (left)

directional conjugate

"you (plural) pay me"

directional conjugate

"I pay you (plural, right and left)

directional conjugate

"you pay us"

directional conjugate

"I pay you all"

directional conjugate

"you two pool your money"
"you share the cost"

Notice in the examples above the Palm Orientation is omitted. Only the required detail will be added until the notation is differentiated from other directional conjugates. (ie: "TO TELL" below). Directional conjugates would need to be collected and recorded in a "Root Verbs" notation chart to ensure clear standardized notation.

handshape, location

directional verb

root verb: "TO PAY"

SAMPLE ROOT VERBS:

root verb: "TO CALL"

root verb: "TO CALL" (2)

root verb: "TO COME/GO

root verb: "TO COME/GO" (one hand)

root verb: "TO DRIVE"

root verb: "TO TELL"

root verb: "TO EMAIL"

root verb: "TO EMAIL" (2)

root verb: "TO GIVE"

root verb: "TO GIVE"

root verb: "TO WALK"

root verb: "TO GIVE" (1 hand)

root verb: "TO HELP"

root verb: "TO SEE"

root verb: "TO TEACH"

CROSS-OVER LOCATIONS

"BEAR"

When the D HS is on the opposite side of the signing space:

When the ND HS is on the opposite side of the signing space:

When both hands cross over to the opposite side of their standard signing side, you can notate it either using:

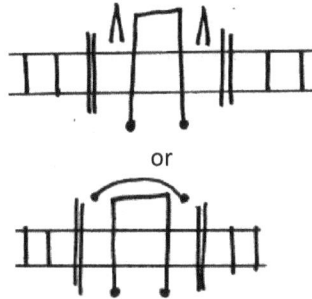

or

"CHINA"

"HAPPY"
"PLEASED" (TO MEET YOU)

Some signs, such as "BEAR" and "LOVE" can use the movement notation "XX" to indicate a crossed arm or hand position:

"LOVE"
"ADORE"
"CARE DEEPLY ABOUT"

Note: The mirror movement symbol can be deleted from movements that are two handed. Ie:

"LOVE"

EMBEDDED MOVEMENTS

EXTERNAL PATH/PRIMARY MOVEMENT

INTERNAL 2ND MOVEMENT

The internal and external movements can be notated. For example:

"SNOW"

"SNOW"
(MIRROR NOTATION)

The internal movement is assumed to be repeating continuously, unless otherwise noted, throughout the external movement as in this sign for snowing:

"SNOW" (CURVY)

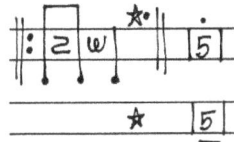

"SNOW" (CURVY)
(MIRROR NOTATION)

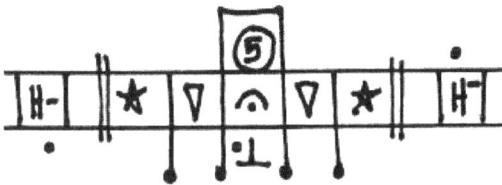

"HURRICANE"

NOTE: The external pathway can be articulated many ways, this is just one variation.

"BUTTERFLY"

FINGERSPELLING, NUMBERS AND DATES

Fingerspelling, numbers, dates, and loan sign are all recorded on the second tier, mid-signing staff.

John Baker

_(206) 531-7280_

301 Poplar St.

Loan Sign examples:

#Style   #Email   #KILL

HANDSHAPE SHIFT

If a sign occurs in one location, and the only movement is a change in handshape, a handshape shift notation can be used:

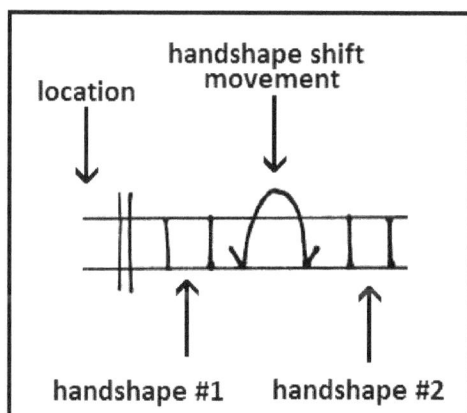

143

ASL: "DO-DO"
"WHAT ARE YOU DOING?"
"TO BE BUSY"

"AWFUL"
"TERRIBLE"
"INCREDIBLE"
"UNBELIEVABLE"

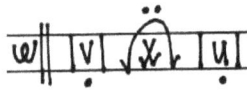

"SCISSORS"

"DOG"
"CANINE"
SPANISH: "PERRO"

"WET"
"MOIST"
"DAMP"

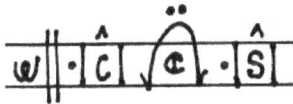

"TOO BAD"
"TOUGH LUCK"

"MILK"

NOTE: Signs that have an "open and close" movement (M:23) can also be written in a standard format:

"MILK"

HEAD NOD AND SHAKE

Shorthand notation for a head nod or shake can be notated on the MVT block, which incorporates these important grammatical components with the sign movement articulation:

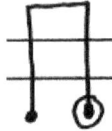　　

HEAD NOD　　　　HEAD SHAKE

MIRROR MVTS

Many signs are made with identical handshapes doing the same movement simultaneously in the same relative location along the Midline Plane:

IDENTICAL MIRROR MVTS

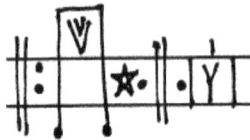　

"PLAY"

"GAME"

NOTE: A different articulation of the sign play cannot be written as a mirror movement as it has different palm orientations:

"PLAY" (2)

CONVERGENT/DIVERGENT MIRROR MVTS

Mirror movements that converge or diverge can be notated to alert the reader to this feature. Here is a sample of a convergent mirror movement:

147

"HURT"
"PAIN"

"COMPUTER"

NOTE: Some movements, as in the signs "FAMILY" and "LOVE", are **default two handed movements** and the mirror notation can be eliminated as redundant. ie:

"FAMILY"

PERSON-MARKER

PERSON-MARKER NOTATION

Here is a sample notation of the ASL verb "teach":

"TEACHER"

"TEACHER"
(MIRROR NOTATION)

"INTERPRETER"

PRONOUNS

Signed languages use pronouns both formal and informal, along with the reflexive ("self") pronoun. These can be notated efficiently by including directionality to conjugate:

	INFORMAL	FORMAL
Personal pronoun (I, me, you, she, he, it, we, they)		
Possessive pronoun (my, your, her, his, its, our, their)		
Reflexive pronoun (myself, yourself, herself, himself, itself, ourselves, yourselves)		

DIRECTIONALITY OF PRONOUNS

YOU	ME	HE, SHE, IT	HE, SHE, IT	YOU ALL	WE	THEY (R)	THEY (L)
⊥	T	Y	⋎	⊥	⌣	ʅ	ʖ

NOTE: Directionality is from the signer's perspective.

SAMPLE PRONOUNS:

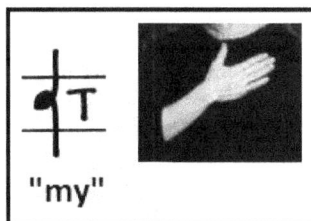

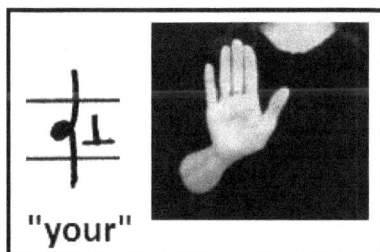

"me" or "I"

"my"

"myself"

"me" or "I" (formal)

"you"

"your"

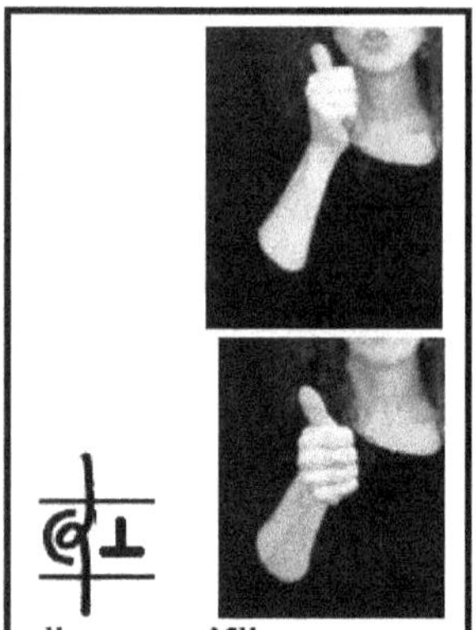

"yourself"

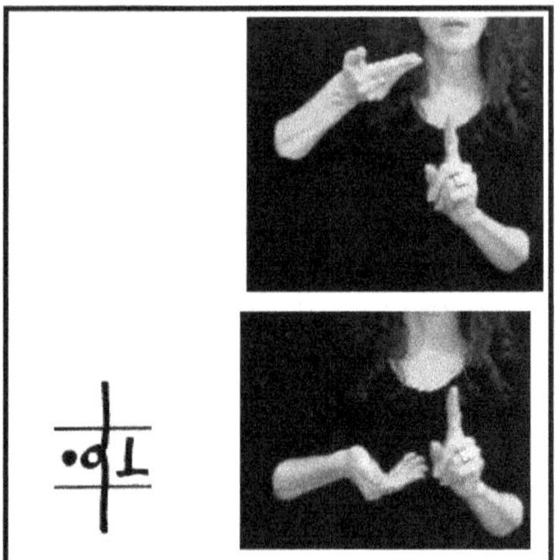

"you" (formal)

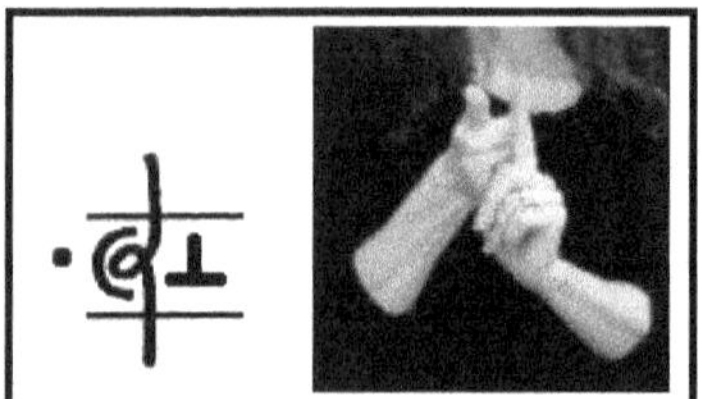

"yourself"
(formal)

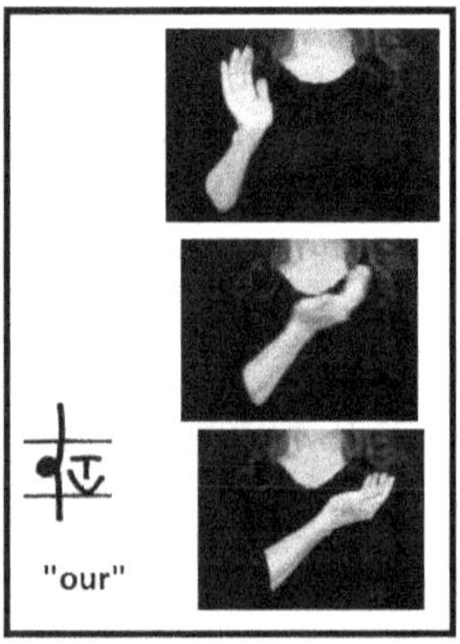

"our"

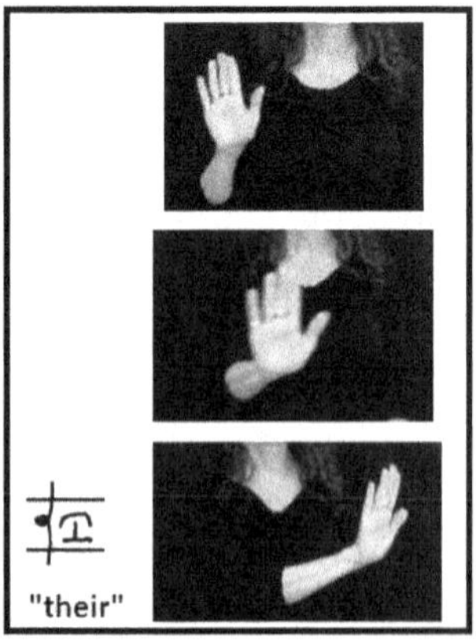

"their"

"her, his, its"

"herself, himself, itself"

"himself, herself, itself"
(formal)

"MY NAME IS DAVE."

PROXIMAL LOCATIONS

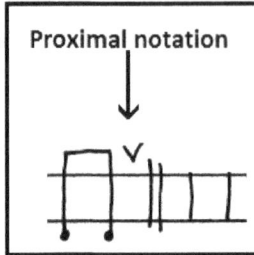

To indicate a sign occurs near a location on the body or face, a proximal notation is needed to clearly separate contact signs (default for face and body locations) from non-contact but proximal signs.

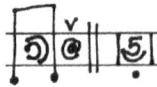

"BEAUTIFUL"
"LOVELY"
"PRETTY"
"GORGEOUS"

SEPARATION OF SIGNS IN A PHRASE

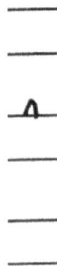

SEPARATION OF SIGNS

Here is a sample notation of the ASL WH ? "Your Mom, where?" (English: "Where is your Mom?"):

"YOUR MOM, WHERE?"

Yₑₛ, Nₒ

The movement symbols for "yes" and "no" can be used on the top tier of the sign staff as a shorthand notation for these common terms:

"yes"

"no"

LISTING

"LET ME COUNT THE WAYS..."

GENERIC LISTING on FIRST TIER (LISTING BLOCK)

Typically the ND HS of an open "5" facing the signer is used as the listing template, and the D HS interacts to express the specific type of list intended. Default ND HS is a "5". A different ND base listing HS can be notated as needed. The following are examples of common forms of listing. There are many more.

ND "5" HS

INDEX TOUCH

Start with the full number (ie: 3) and touch each one on fingertip using a bent index HS.

NUMBERING

To denote the number of items in the generic list, **notate the number over listing block**. This applies to all subsequent listing types.

INDEX
AIR COUNT

Start with the full number (ie: 2) and "air count" each number using a bent index HS and a "bouncing" counting motion.

1

2

3

INDEX
AIR SWEEP

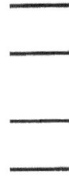

Broad general air-sweep" using a bent index HS.

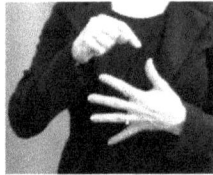

INDEX DRAG

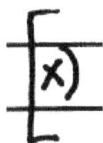

Index drags down across the ND list hand.

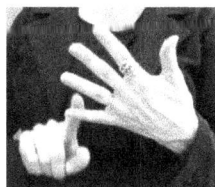

FLIP TOUCH

Each finger flips out one at a time and is touched on the fingertip as you count: 1,2,3,4,5

FLIP BOUNCE

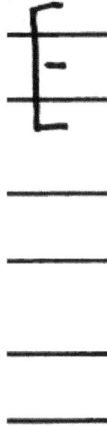

There is no base listing HS. The listing is with one hand and has a bouncing movement between each flip.

CHOP TOUCH

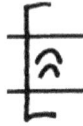

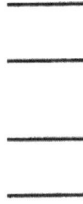

Start with the full number (ie: 5) and touch each finger with the "bent B with thumb extended" or bent base handshape as you work thru the list in a bouncing or "chopping" motion.

AIR CHOP

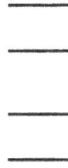

This is the same as the previous listing example, but without touching the base listing hand.

CHOP SWEEP

EITHER

TWIST

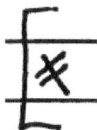

___

___

___

___

1ST

2ND

3RD

AIR SPIRAL

MOUSE CLICK

*VARIATION
Can also use
"CHECK-LIST"
notation
with
"checking off"
movement

PALM SWEEP

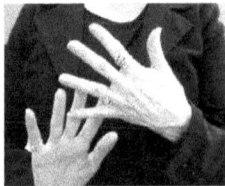

ASL-FIST LIST

SPECIFIC LISTING

To create a list of actual items (ie: dog, cat, fish), the notation needs to shift to the **grammar block** on the second tier, with identification of the type of list being initiated. Then list the first specific item: (for example the color "red" in a series of colors), with subsequent items numbered in the listed series:

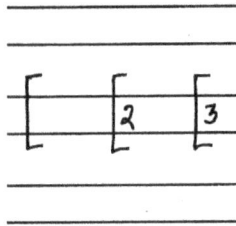

SPECIFIC LISTING on SECOND TIER

Let's look at an actual example. The signer mentions an upcoming list (generic), and then proceeds to create the list of specific named items:

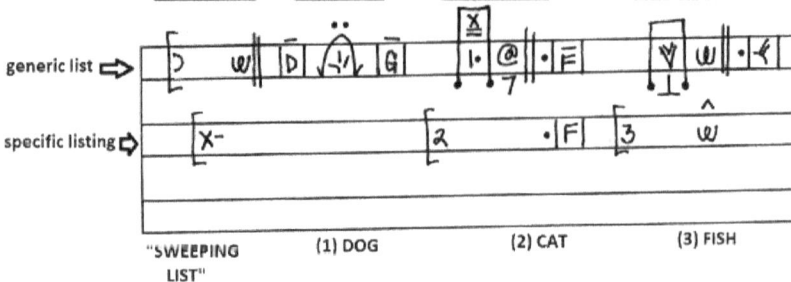

generic list ➡

specific listing ➡

"SWEEPING LIST"   (1) DOG   (2) CAT   (3) FISH

Here is another example using a different listing type.

specific list ⟹

(1) "WATER"   (2) "MILK "   (3) "COFFEE"

Note: the first specific listing notation is count "1" and the numbering begins 2, 3, 4, 5, etc... The total anticipated number of items can bee notated above the initial notation as in the example above that had a list of three types of beverages. This alerts the reader to anticipate the total number of upcoming items.

173

SIGN-TO-TEXT
ACADEMIC THESAURUS

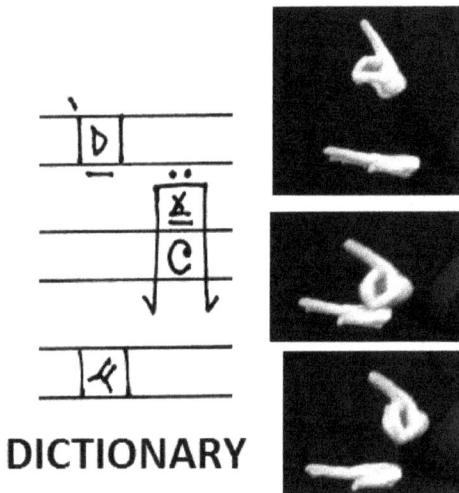

DICTIONARY

Imagine school children having independent access to a sign-to-text bilingual academic thesaurus or dictionary resource. The sample terms listed below are in English alphabetical order. Future signotation thesauri would be organized according to the 5 Parameters within sections (Base Handshape Pairs, Alternating Handshapes, Mirror Movements, Handshape Shift, Compound Signs, etc...) enabling users to search for a sign and find equivalent second language terms for academic enrichment. Benefits include the ability to start with a given sign, locate the desired term and check for spelling as well as synonyms, antonyms and trilingual terms.

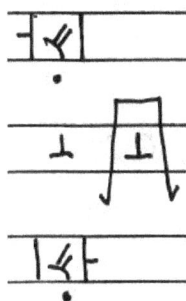

"AFTER"
"SUBSEQUENT"

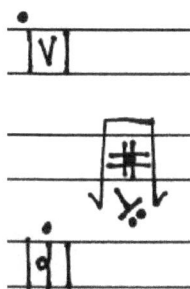

"APPLY"
"APPLICATION"

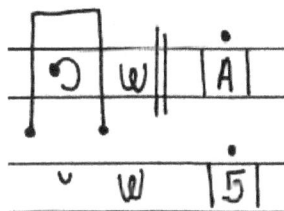

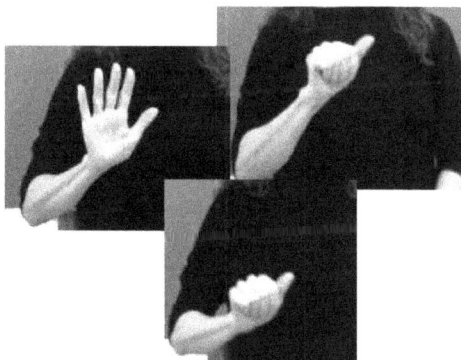

"ASIA"

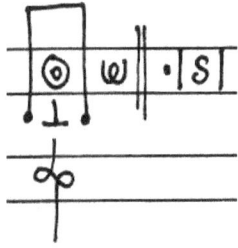

"ASL"

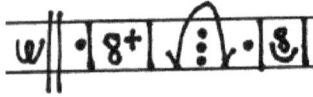

"AWFUL"
"TERRIBLE"
"INCREDIBLE"
"UNBELIEVABLE"

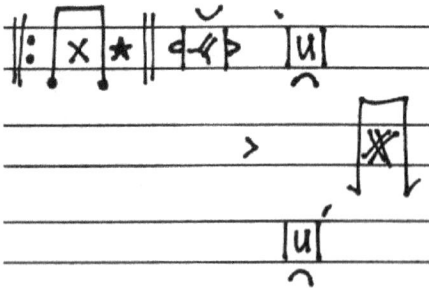

"BABYSIT"
"CHILDCARE"

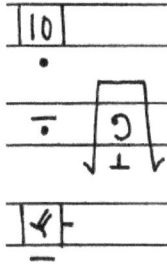

"BASEMENT"
"UNDERNEATH"

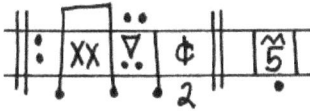

"BEAR"

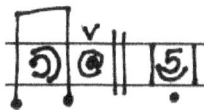

"BEAUTIFUL"
"LOVELY"
"PRETTY"
"GORGEOUS"

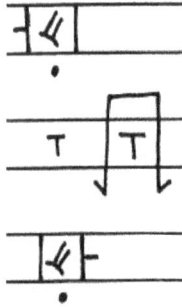

"BEFORE"
"PRIOR"
"AHEAD OF TIME"

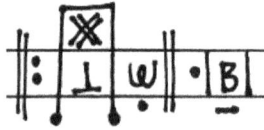

"BLOCK"
"PREVENT"
"BARRIER"
"OBSTACLE"
"THWART"

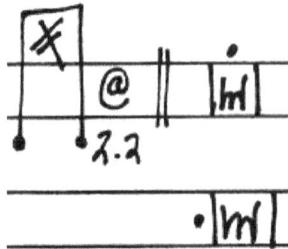

"BORING"

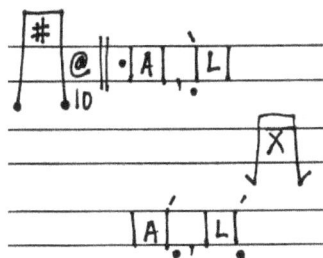

"BROTHER"

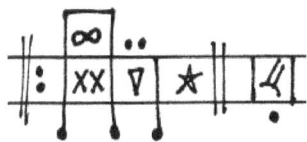

"BUTTERFLY"

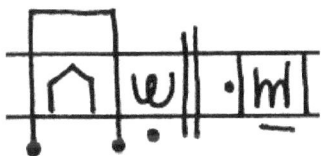

"CAMP"
"TENT"

179

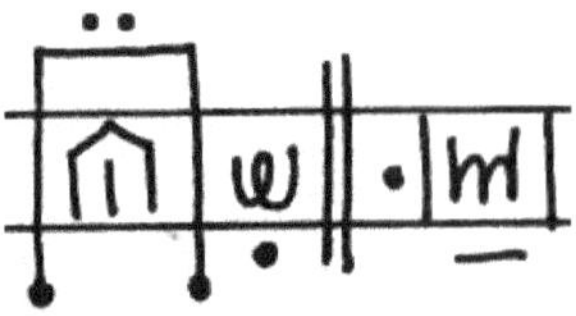

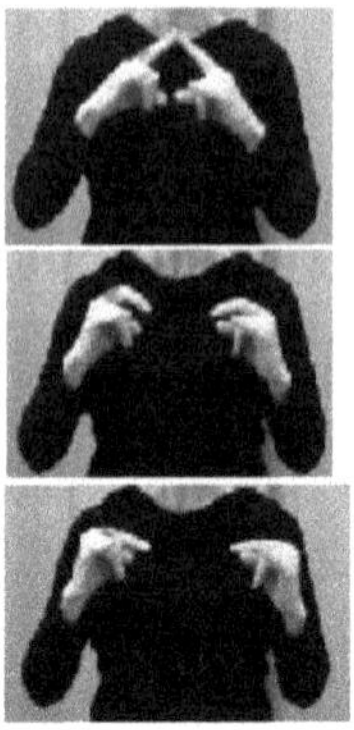

"CAMPING"

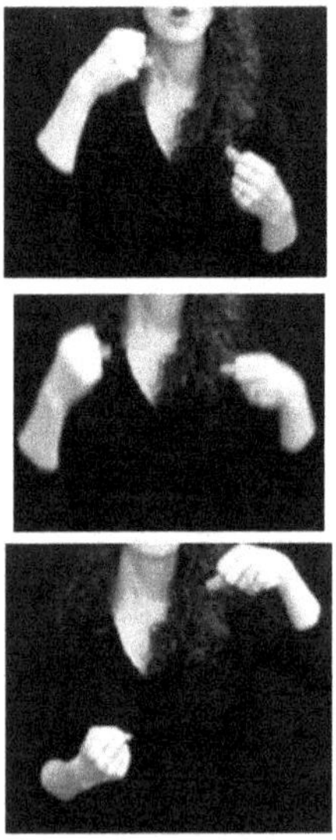

"CAR"
"AUTOMOBILE"

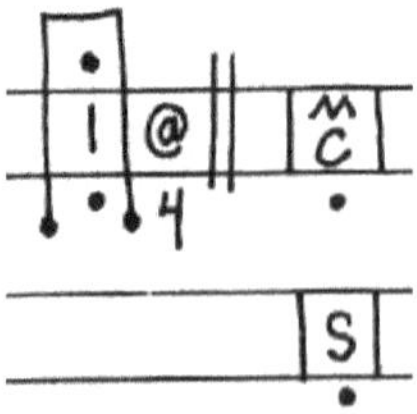

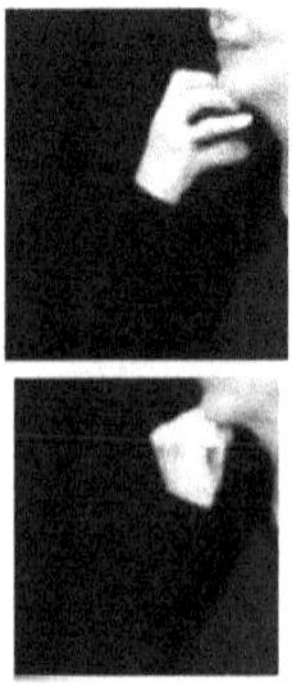

"CHERISH"
"ADORE"
"VALUE"

"CHINA"

"COFFEE"

"COMPUTER"

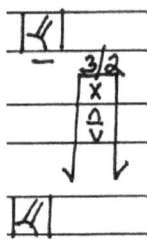
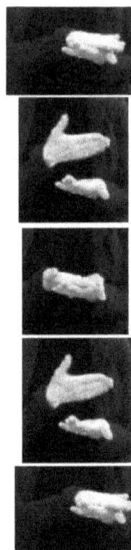

"COOK"

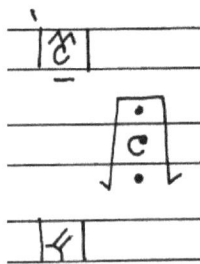
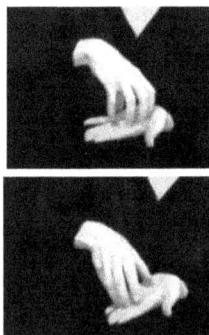

"COOKIE"

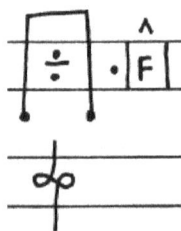
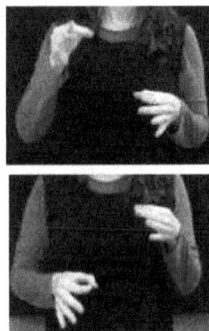

"COURT"

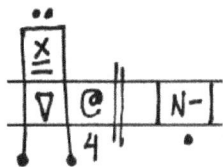

"CUTE"
"DARLING"
"ADORABLE"

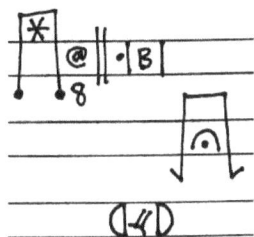

"DAUGHTER"

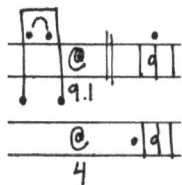

"DEAF"

ASL: "DO-DO"
"WHAT ARE YOU DOING?"
"TO BE BUSY"

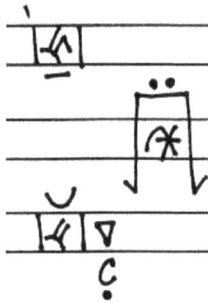

"DOCTOR"
"PHYSICIAN"

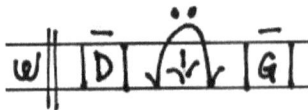

"DOG"
"CANINE"
SPANISH: "PERRO"

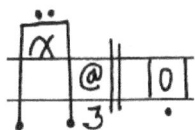

"EAT"
"HAVE A BITE TO EAT"
"CONSUME"
"MUNCH"
"INHALE"
"GOBBLE"
"SCARF IT DOWN"

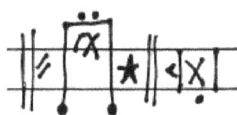

"ELECTRIC"
"ELECTRICITY"
"BATTERY"

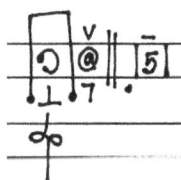

"EMBARRASSED"

Related terms: "MORTIFIED"
"CHAGRINED"
"HUMILIATED"

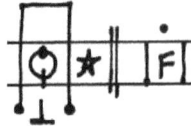

"FAMILY"

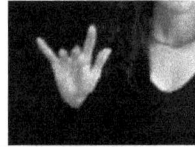
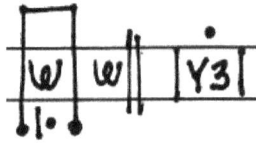

"FINGERSPELL"
"FINGERSPELLING"

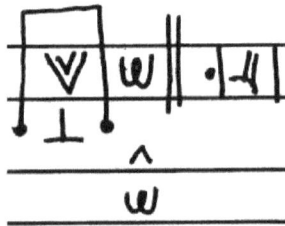

"FISH"

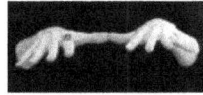

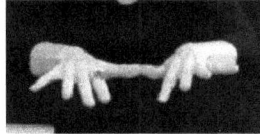

"FLIRT"

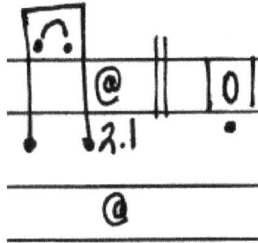

"FLOWER"
"POSY"

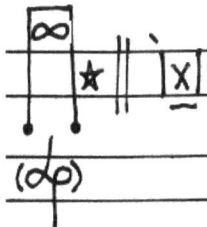

"FRIEND"

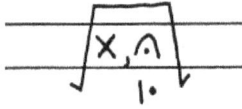

"FROM"

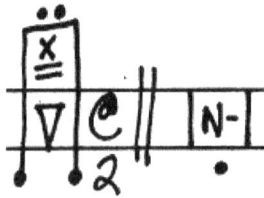

"FUNNY"
"AMUSING"

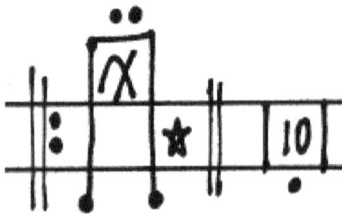

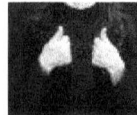

"GAME"

"GIRLFRIEND"

"HAPPY BIRTHDAY"

189

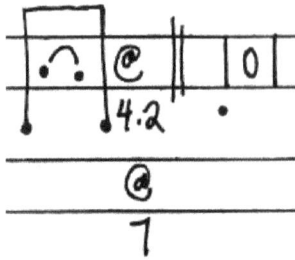 

"HOME"

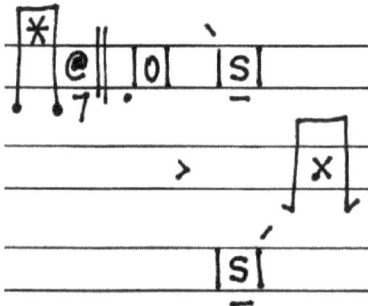 

"HOMEWORK"
"ASSIGNMENT"

"HOUSE"

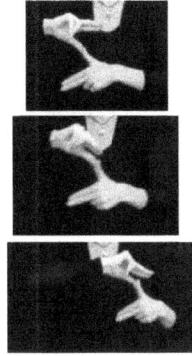

"HURRICANE"

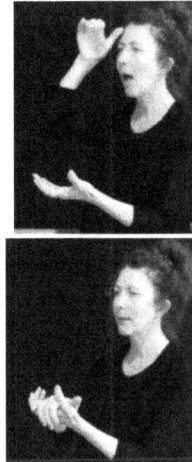

"HUSBAND"

"ILLEGAL"
"PROHIBITED"
"FORBIDDEN"
"UNLAWFUL"
"AGAINST THE RULES"

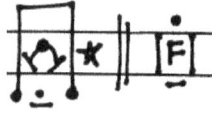

"IMPORTANT"
"CRITICAL"
"VITAL"

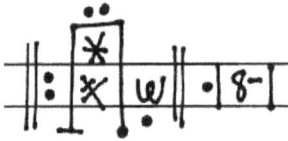

"ONLINE"
"INTERNET"

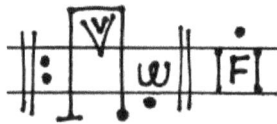

"INTERPRET"

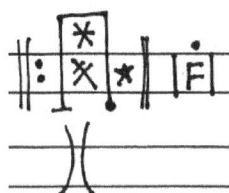

"INTERPRETER"

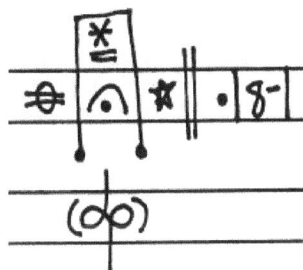

"JESUS"

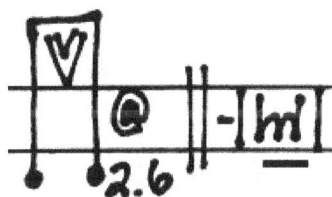

"KID"

193

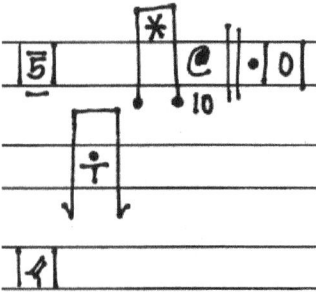 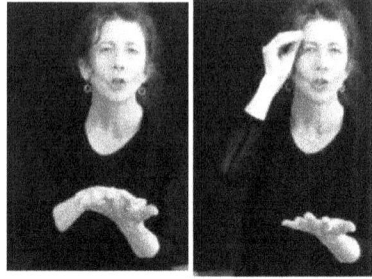

"LEARN"

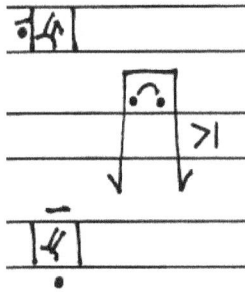 

"LESSON"

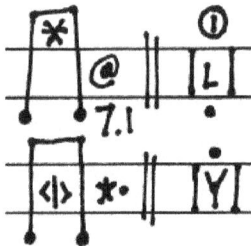 

"LOOK LIKE"
"RESEMBLE"
"SIMILAR"

194

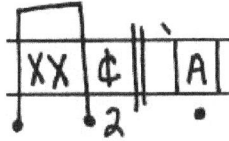 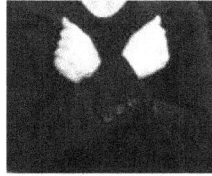

"LOVE"
"ADORE"
"CARE DEEPLY ABOUT"

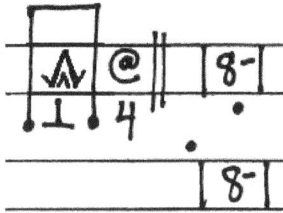 

"LUCKY" / "LUCK"
"FORTUNATE"
"FORTUITOUS"

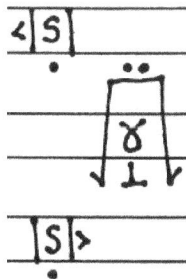 

"MAKE"
"MANUFACTURE"
"PRODUCE"
"CREATE"

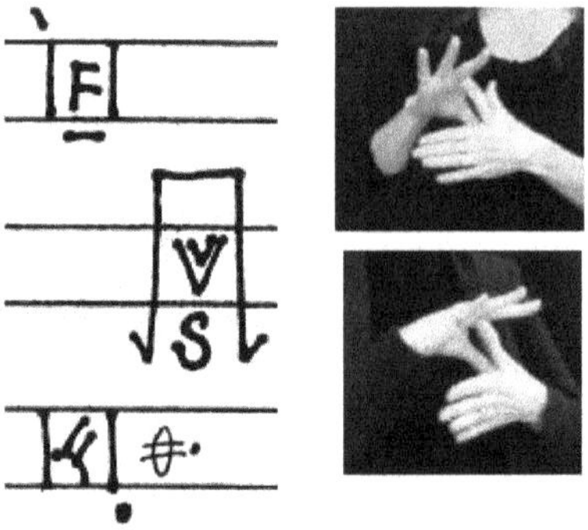

"MEAT"
"CONTENT" (SUBJECT)

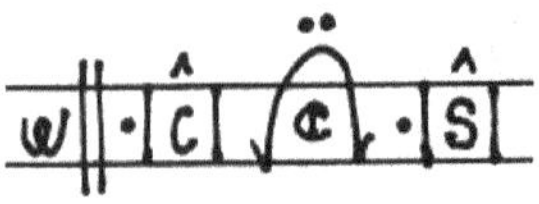
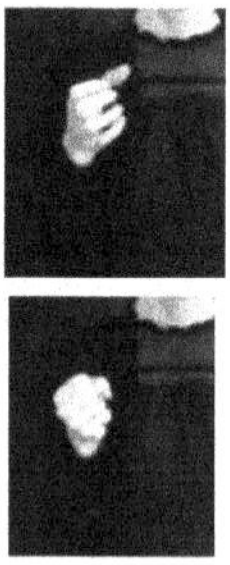

"MILK"

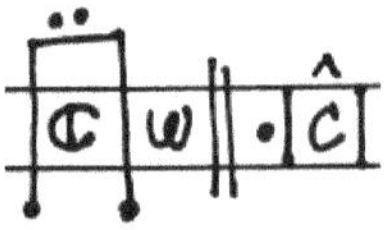
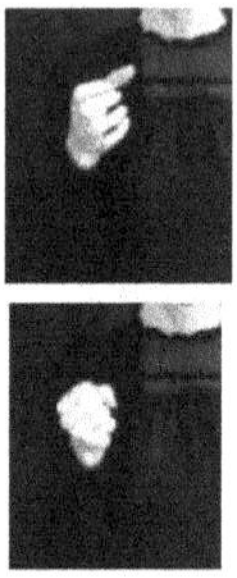

"MILK"

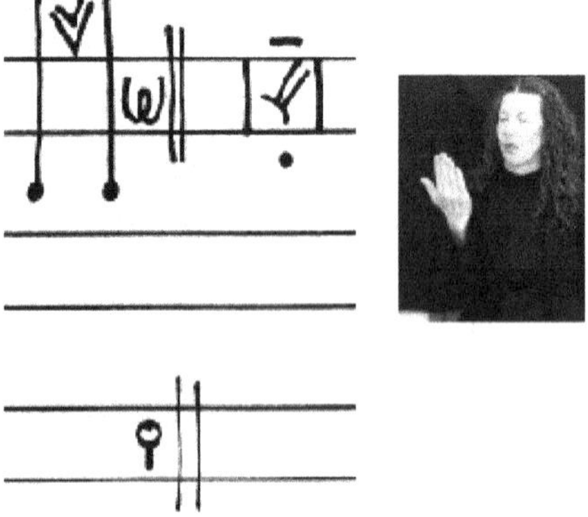

"MIRROR"

"NAME"

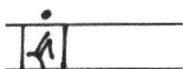

"NEW"

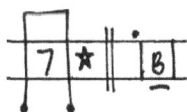
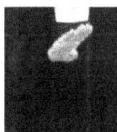

"NEVER"

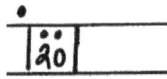

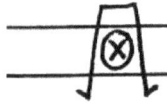

"NEWSPAPER"

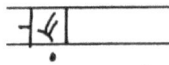

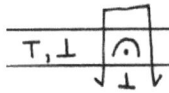

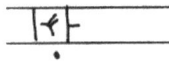

"NEXT"
"THEN"
"ADJACENT"

"no"

"NUMBER"

"OFTEN"

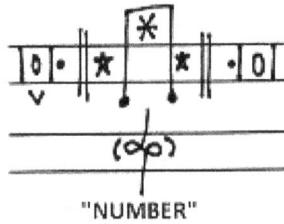

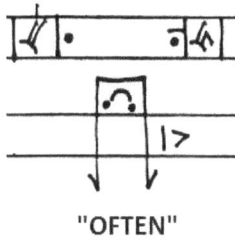

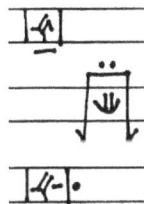

"ON THE FENCE"
"UNCERTAIN"
"INDECISIVE"
"AMBIVALENT"
"EQUIVOCATE"

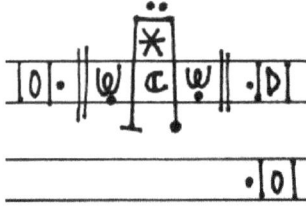

"ONE MORE"

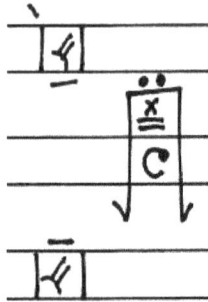

"PAPER"

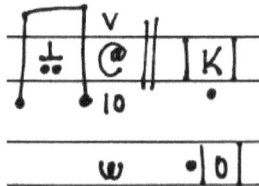

"PASS OUT"
(EITHER IN SLEEP OR BLACK OUT)
"UNCONSCIOUS"

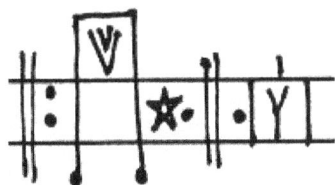 

"PLAY"

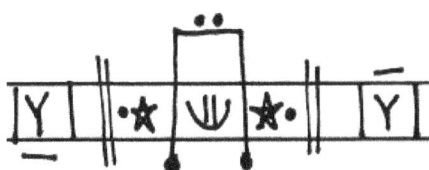  

"PLAY" (2)

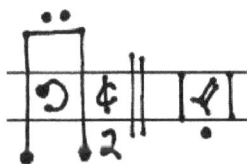 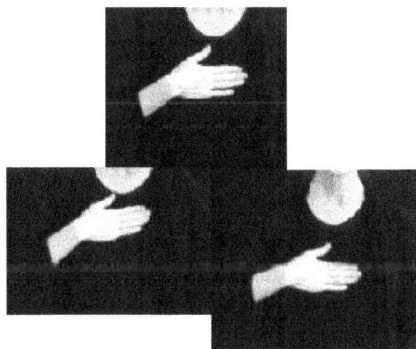

"PLEASE"

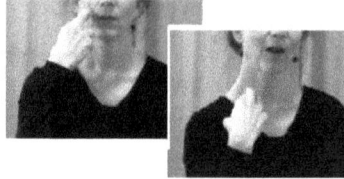

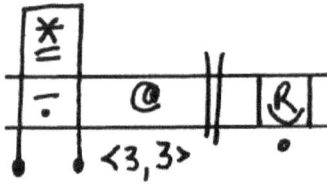

"RESTAURANT"

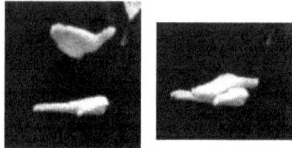

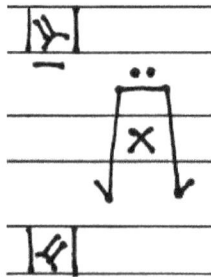

"SCHOOL"
"ACADEMIC"

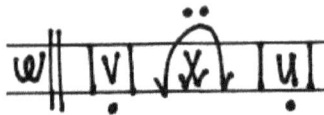

"SCISSORS"

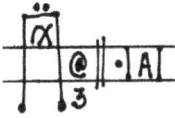 

"SECRET"
"PRIVATE"
"PASS" (WORD)
"CLANDESTINE"
"CONFIDENTIAL"

OR

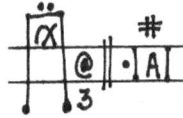 

"SECRET"
"PRIVATE"
"PASS" (WORD)
"CLANDESTINE"
"CONFIDENTIAL"

(THUMBNAIL LOCATION)

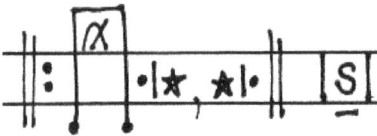

"SHOE"

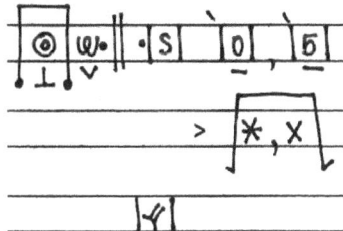

"SIGNOTATION"

"SISTER"

"SON"

"SORRY"
"APOLOGIZE"
"REGRET"

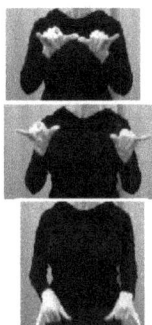

"SYSTEM"

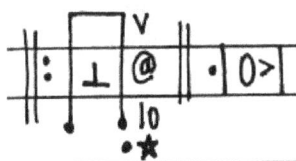

"TEACHER"
(MIRROR NOTATION)

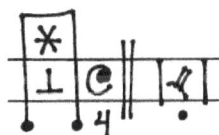

"THANK YOU"

"TIME"

"TIME" (2)

"TIME" (2)
FORWARD LOCATION

"TOO BAD"
"TOUGH LUCK"

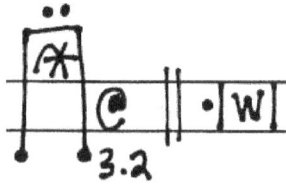

"WATER"

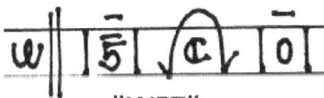

"WET"
"MOIST"
"DAMP"

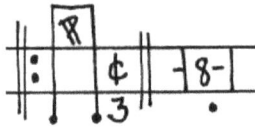

"WHAT'S UP"

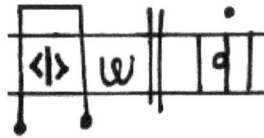

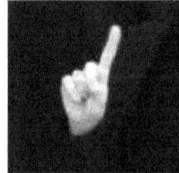

"WHERE ?"

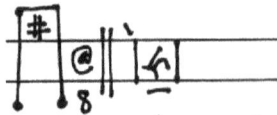

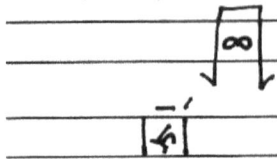

"WIFE"

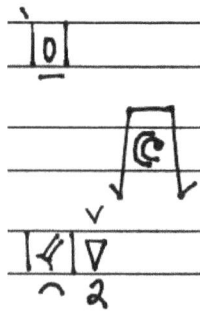

"X-RAY: WRIST"

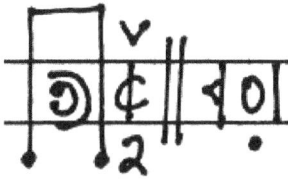

"X-RAY: CHEST"

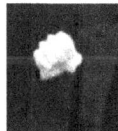

"yes"

SPREAD THE SIGN: INTERNATIONAL SIGNS IN SIGNOTATION

One of the most fun and exciting aspects of a system like signotation is the ability to apply these principles to any sign language globally. For example, the website "Spread the Sign" has examples of signs from all over the world for common terms. Here is the signotation version for "computer" in 5 languages. You can find the source signs by clicking on the flag for the related country by the entry "computer". Experiment with your own signotations for other international signs!

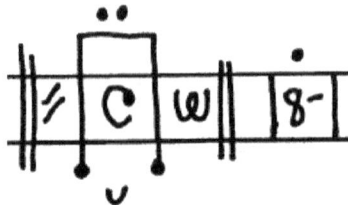

"COMPUTER" ~ASL

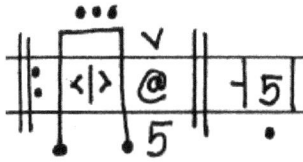

"COMPUTER" ~Japanese

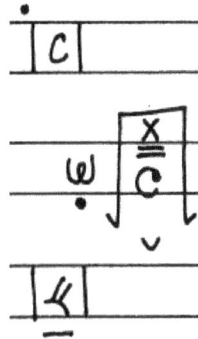

"COMPUTER" ~Russian

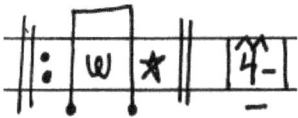

"COMPUTER" ~Italian

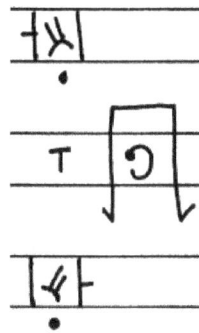

"COMPUTER" ~Lithuanian

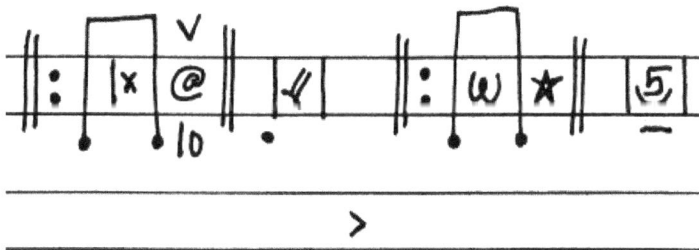

"COMPUTER" ~Finnish

WHAT ABOUT CLASSIFIERS/DEPICTING VERBS?

Classifiers or "depicting verbs" are an important and integral part of ASL and will be the subject of a separate book dedicated to exploring this unique linguistic feature of signed languages.

WRITE YOUR OWN SIGNOTATIONS!

THE 5 PARAMETERS
SIGNOTATION
~CHARTS~

1. Handshape (HS)

2. Palm Orientation (PO)

3. Location (LOC)

4. Movement (MVT)

5. Facial grammar (NMGM)

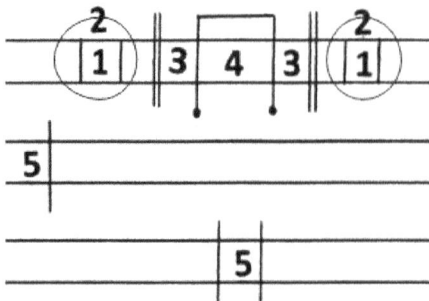

(P1) ASL SN HANDSHAPES

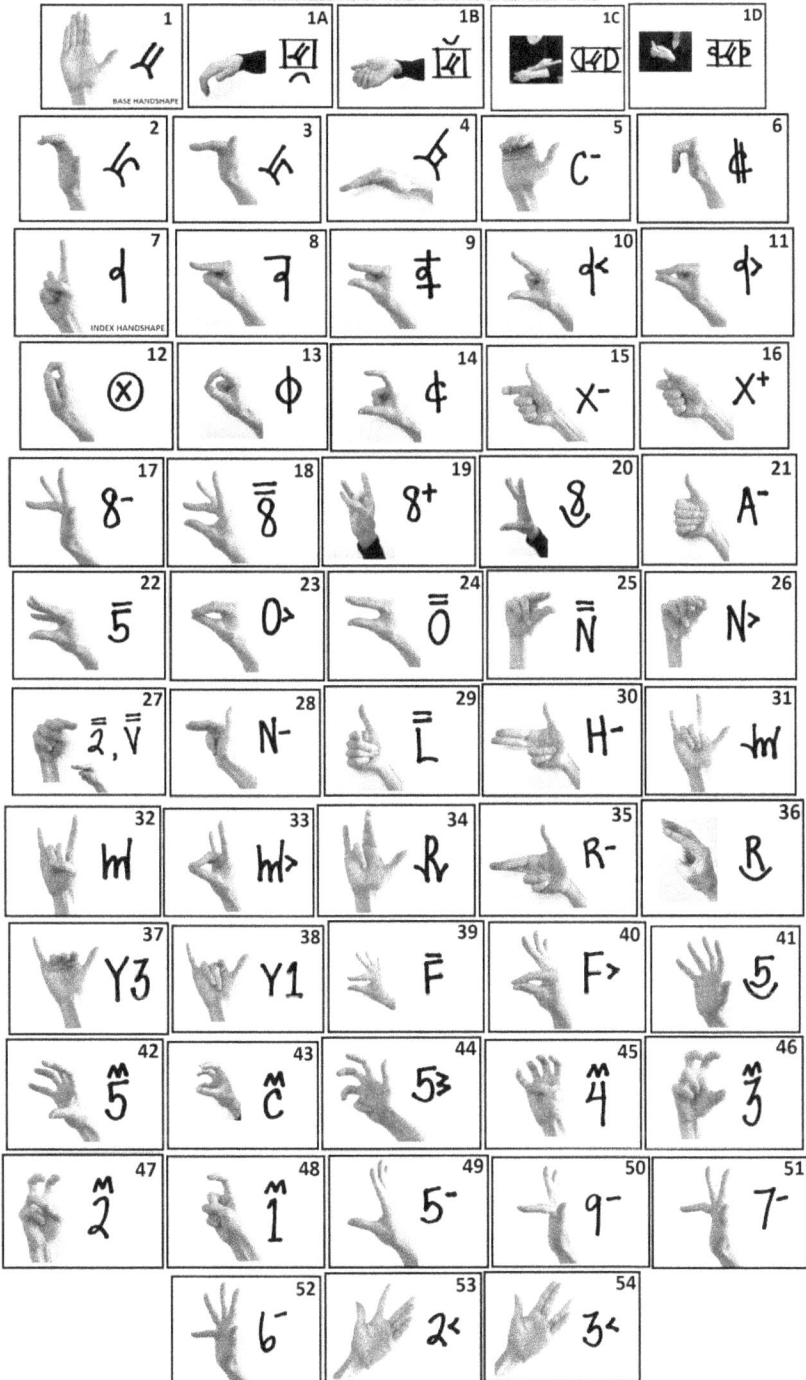

1 𝓎 BASE HANDSHAPE	**1A**	**1B**	**1C**	**1D**
2	**3**	**4**	**5** C⁻	**6** ¢
7 ꝙ INDEX HANDSHAPE	**8**	**9** ₮	**10** ⊲	**11** ⊳
12 ⊗	**13** φ	**14** ¢	**15** X⁻	**16** X⁺
17 8⁻	**18** 8̿	**19** 8⁺	**20** 8	**21** A⁻
22 5̄	**23** O⊃	**24** Ō̄	**25** N̄	**26** N⊃
27 2̿, V̄	**28** N⁻	**29** L̄	**30** H⁻	**31** ₥
32 ₥	**33** ₥⊃	**34** ℛ	**35** R⁻	**36** ℛ
37 Y3	**38** Y1	**39** F̄	**40** F⊃	**41** 5
42 5̃	**43** C̃	**44** 5̃⊃	**45** 4̃	**46** 3̃
47 2̃	**48** 1̃	**49** 5⁻	**50** 9⁻	**51** 7⁻
52 6⁻	**53** 2⊲	**54** 3⊲		

(P2) ASL SN PALM ORIENTATION

BASIC PO {R,L,F,B}   ANGLED PO

PO down to the ground: "CHILD"

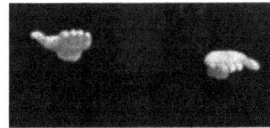

PO Up to the sky: "MAYBE"

PO TO THE MIDLINE   PO SETTING 1   PO SETTING 2

FINGERTIP DIRECTION

fingertips angled inward   fingertips angled outward

45 DEGREE TILT

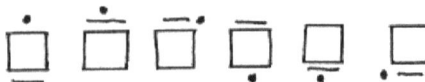

(P3) ASL SN LOCATIONS

6 BASIC LOCATIONS:

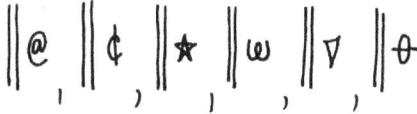

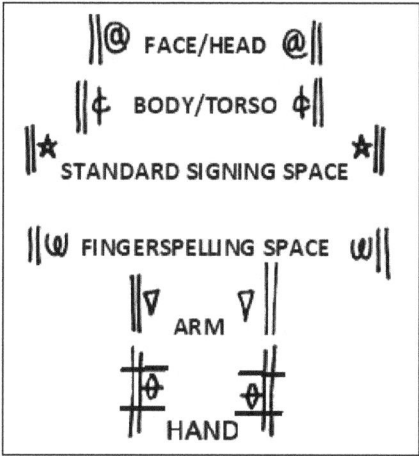

$\|@_,\ \|¢_)\ \|\star_)\ \|ω_)\ \|\triangledown_)\ \|\theta$

||@ FACE/HEAD @||

||¢ BODY/TORSO ¢||

||★ STANDARD SIGNING SPACE ★||

||ω FINGERSPELLING SPACE ω||

||∇ ARM ∇||

╫θ ╫θ HAND

||@ FACE/HEAD LOCATIONS @||

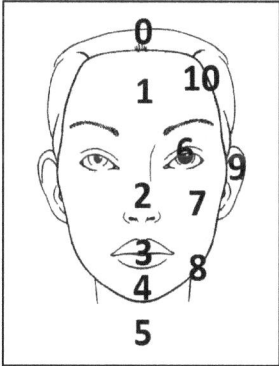

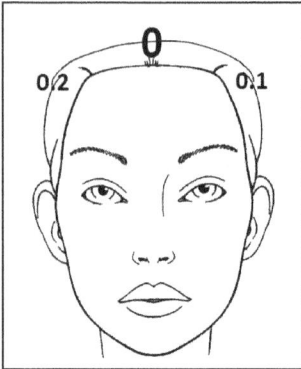

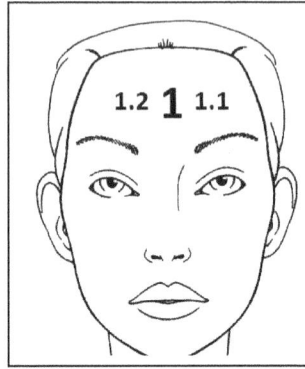

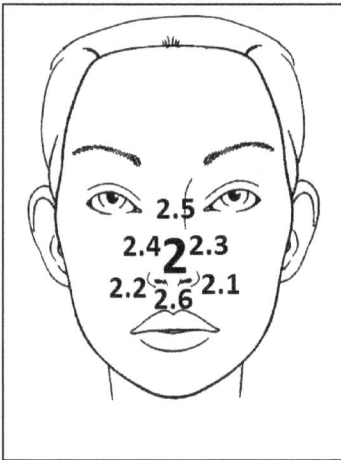

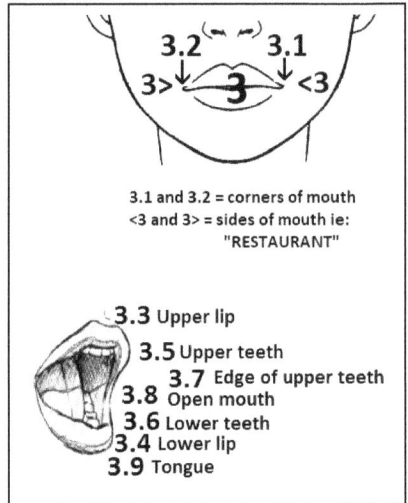

3.1 and 3.2 = corners of mouth
<3 and 3> = sides of mouth ie:
"RESTAURANT"

3.3 Upper lip
3.5 Upper teeth
3.7 Edge of upper teeth
3.8 Open mouth
3.6 Lower teeth
3.4 Lower lip
3.9 Tongue

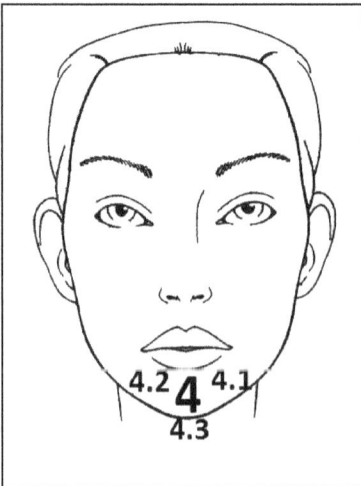

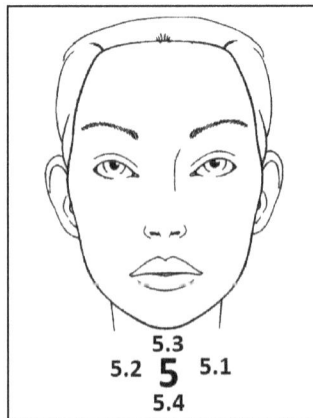

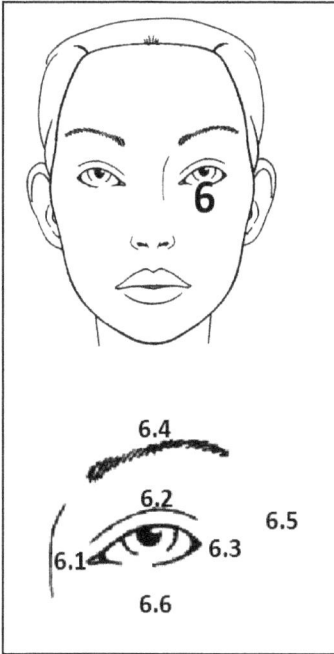

6.4
6.2
6.5
6.1
6.3
6.6

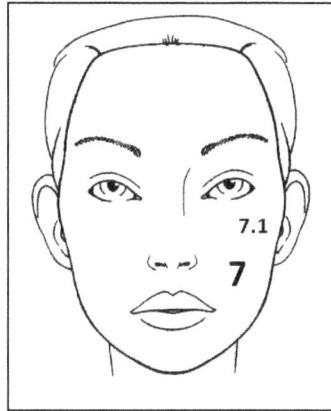

7.1
7

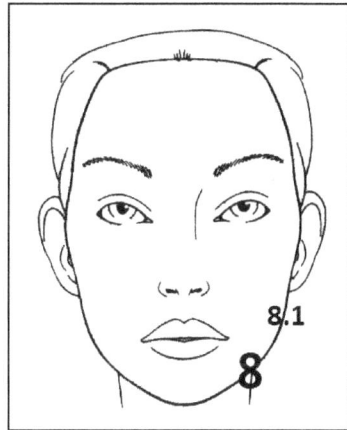

8.1
8

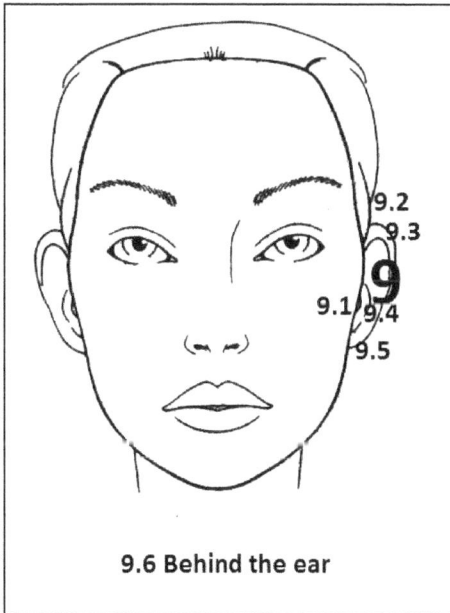

9.2
9.3
9
9.1
9.4
9.5

9.6 Behind the ear

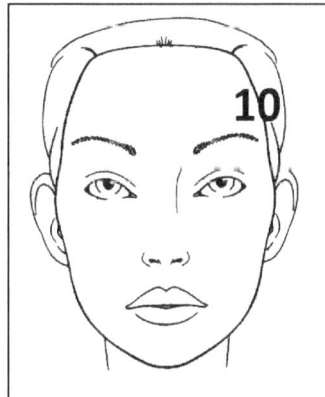

10

||¢ **TORSO LOCATIONS** ¢||

30		20
3	2	1
6	5	4
9	8	7
12	11	10

VERTICAL LOCATIONS #1-5

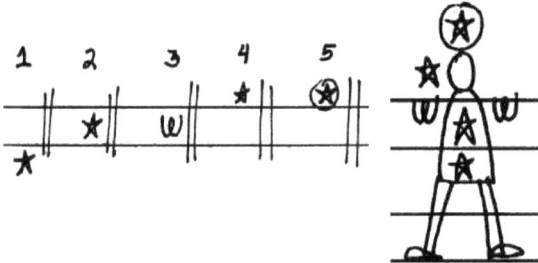

Standard Signing Spaces and Fingerspelling Space

LATERAL LOCATIONS

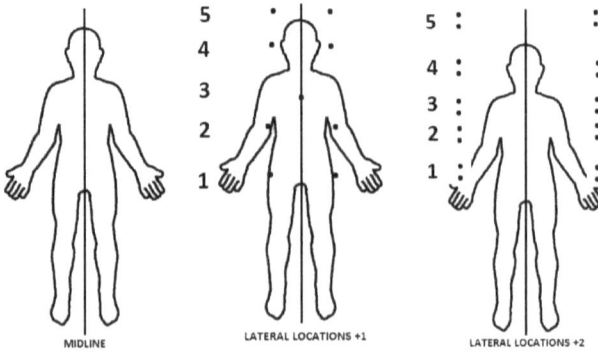

MIDLINE   LATERAL LOCATIONS +1   LATERAL LOCATIONS +2

HORIZONTAL LOCATIONS

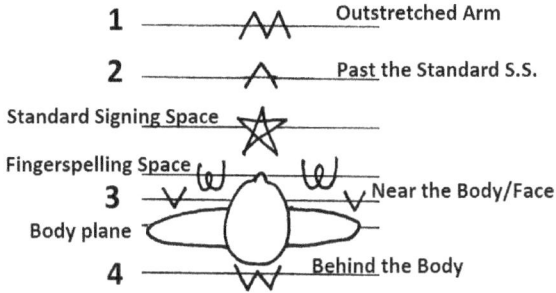

1 — Outstretched Arm
2 — Past the Standard S.S.
Standard Signing Space
Fingerspelling Space
3 — Near the Body/Face
Body plane
4 — Behind the Body

SIDE LOCATION

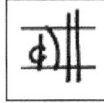

ARMPIT LOCATION

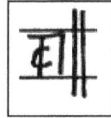

HIP LOCATION

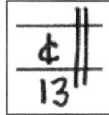

ADDITIONAL BODY LOCATIONS

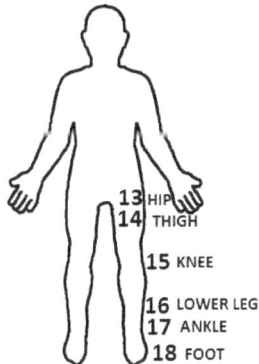

13 HIP
14 THIGH
15 KNEE
16 LOWER LEG
17 ANKLE
18 FOOT

THE ARM AND HAND

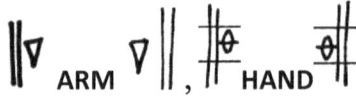

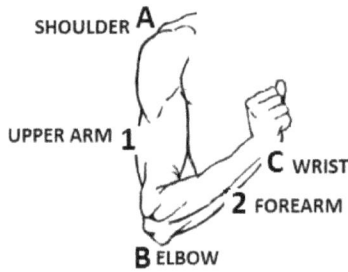

ARM , HAND

SHOULDER **A**

UPPER ARM **1**

C WRIST

2 FOREARM

B ELBOW

HAND AND FINGER IDENTIFICATION

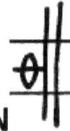

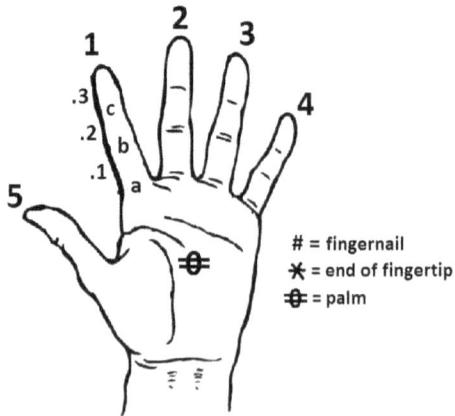

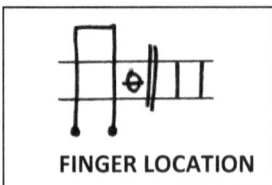

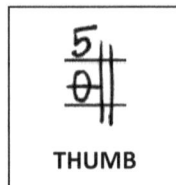

1 2 3

4

.3 c

.2 b

.1 a

5

\# = fingernail
✳ = end of fingertip
⊕ = palm

FINGER LOCATION

5

THUMB

THE PALM

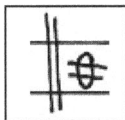

NON DOMINANT

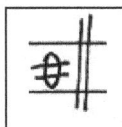

DOMINANT

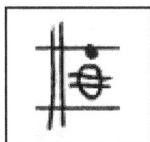

TOP SURFACE OF THE PALM (Back of the hand) IE: "WARRANT"

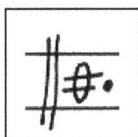

INSIDE EDGE OF ND PALM IE: "MEAT"

THE FOUR FACES OF THE ARM

"DUTY" LOC

"DOCTOR" LOC

"CYST ON WRIST" (INSIDE)

"CYST ON WRIST" (OUTSIDE)

(P4) ASL SN MOVEMENTS

DM:1 UP NORTH, TALL, ROCKET LIFT-OFF	**DM:2** DOWN SOUTH, THIRSTY, SNOW	**DM:3** RIGHT EAST/WEST, PERSON WALKS R	**DM:4** LEFT EAST/WEST, PERSON WALKS L	**DM:5** AWAY FROM SIGNER I-GIVE-YOU, DRIVE STRAIGHT AHEAD
DM:6 TOWARDS SIGNER YOU-PAY-ME PERSON APPROACHES ME	**DM:7** AWAY FROM SIGNER (L) EVICT/DEPORT (L)	**DM:8** AWAY FROM SIGNER (R) COMMUTE TO WORK (R)	**DM:9** TOWARDS SIGNER (L) SHE-HELPS-ME (FROM L)	**DM:10** TOWARDS SIGNER (R) HE-EMAILS-ME (FROM R)
DM:11 DIAGONAL: UP + LEFT ROCKET DIAGONAL L	**DM:12** DIAGONAL: UP + RIGHT ROCKET DIAGONAL R	**DM:13** DIAGONAL: DOWN + LEFT UGLY (L HAND)	**DM:14** DIAGONAL: DOWN + RIGHT UGLY (R HAND)	**DM:19** SIDE TO SIDE HORIZONTALLY TRAVEL TO AND FRO
DM:20 UP AND DOWN VERTICALLY ELEVATOR	**DM: 18** UPWARD ANGLE LEARN	**DM:17** DOWNWARD ANGLE KNOCKED OUT, UNCONSCIOUS	**DM:16** DOWNWARD WITH FORCE BANKRUPT	**FM:1** WIGGLE COLOR, SNOW
FM:2 FLICK TOO BAD, HATE, FEEDBACK	**FM:3** SCISSOR SHEEP, HAIRCUT	**FM:4** SNAP DOG	**FM:5** PINCH MEAT, SKIN	**FM:6** WALK WALK AROUND
FM:7 CLIMB WALK UPSTAIRS/DOWNSTAIRS	**FM:8** KNUCKLE BOB MOUSE, RABBIT	**FM:9** FINGER BOB 1X SNAP A PHOTO	**FM:10** SIDE BOB "NO-NO" GESTURE	**FM:11** QUESTION MARK GOVERNMENT, ASK A QUESTION QQ
FM: 12 SQUEEZE IN PLACE REPEATEDLY MAD, SPONGE, WANT, INSECT	**M:1** HOP DOLPHIN, CHILDREN, HARD OF HEARING	**M:2** VIBRATE FISH, PLAY, FOR FOR? MEDICINE, WHERE, MOVIE BLUE, SILLY, FINISH	**M:3** BOUNCE HAT, CHILD	**M:4** WRIST NOD YES, HAVE TO
M:5 CLOCKWISE CIRCLE MONDAY, GESTURE	**M:6** COUNTER-CLOCKWISE CIRCLE SIGNING, ASIA, PLEASE	**M:7** FULL CIRCLE OUTWARD FAMILY	**M:8** FULL CIRCLE INWARD PLACE, AREA	**M:9** ARCS UPWARD GO/COME, RAINBOW
M:10 ARCS DOWNWARD ELEPHANT, WELCOME	**M:11** BACK AND FORTH, SIDE TO SIDE WHAT, ANIMAL, TRAIN, ELEVATOR	**M:12** HS GOES THRU HS GREY, EMAIL	**M:13** HS GOES UNDER HS SNEAK OUT, KICK, HIDE	**M:14** HS ON TOP OF HS CHAMP! PUT ON A CHARACTER

POKE **M:15**	TWIST **M:16**	THROW **M:17**	REVERSE THROW **M:18**	WRIST FLIP **M:19**
OWE 5, TAP FOR ATTENTION	KEY, COOL/NEAT, VOICE OFF	ASL, THROW OUT/GARBAGE	AND, COPY, LEARN, CATCH A BALL	COOK, DIE

WRIST FLIP + ROLL **M:20**	WRIST FLIP FIRM **M:21** 3X	WRIST ROCK SIDE-TO-SIDE **M:22**	HS OPENS AND CLOSES **M:23**	ARCS **M:24**
HOW, HAPPEN	BLUE (FIRM), FINISH	GREEN, ARGUE, CHUBBY, DANCE, WOW	MILK, BIRD, NO	CAR, TRUCK, PARIS

SHAKE **M:25**	SCOOP AND LIFT **M:26**	SOFT "7" **M:27**	PARTIAL CIRCLE **M:28**	SWIRL **M:29**
BATHROOM, WHERE, SIMILAR, BAR	NEW, WHAT'S UP?	NEVER, FUN, CHICAGO	IMPORTANT	BEAUTIFUL, AFRICA, X-RAY

CONTACT **CM:1**	TAPPING **CM:2**	FINGERTIP CONTACT **CM:3**	GLANCE OFF **CM:4**	INTERTWINE CLAMP **CM:5**
SCHOOL, GAME	WARN, CRACKER, DENTIST	BIRTHDAY, EQUAL	PAPER, CLEAN, STAR	MARRIED, HAMBURGER, FRIEND

FINGERS INTERSECT **CM:6**	FINGERS INTERSECT AT BASE **CM:7**	TAPPING FINGERTIP **CM:8**	FINGERS OVERLAP **CM:9**	FINGERTIP GLANCE OFF **CM:10**
AMERICA	PREGNANT, FOOTBALL	FAVORITE, MAMA, MORE	NAME	I-PAD, CAT

HINGE **CM:11**	CROSSED ARMS **CM:12**	FIRM CONTACT **CM:13**	CONTACT + BOUNCE **CM:14**	FIRM CONTACT + BOUNCE **CM:15**
BOOK, PURSE	BEAR, LOVE, REST, SECURE	RIGHT, ESTABLISH	ON-TIME, PRINT	ILLEGAL, TRICK/FOOL

TAP-TAP (2) FINGERTIP FIRM **CM:16**	PARALLEL **CM:17**	APPROACHES WITHOUT CONTACT **CM:18**	KISS **CM:19**	SCRATCH **CM:20**
OWE 5	PARALLEL, HIGHWAY	REDUCE, MEET SOMEONE, NEAR	KISS-FIST	BEAR, ANALYZE, SUSPECT

CONTACT CONTINUOUS **CM:21**	PINCH-PULL **CM:22**	PULL APART **CM:23**	DRAGS **CM:24**	CONTACT, BOUNCE, CONTACT **CM:25**
ROMANCE, EMPHASIZE	VOLUNTEER, HAIR	STORY, SENTENCE	HUNGRY, DEPRESSED, CRY	BIRTHDAY, LESSON, DEAF, HOME, PARENTS

WAVE+DRAGS **CM:26**	CRADLE ARMS **CM:27**	CONTACT + LIP-SWOOP **CM:28**	TWIST + TURN FORWARD **CM:29**	TOUCH, TURN, TOUCH **CM:30**
DRAW PICTURE, METH	DAUGHTER/SON, BABY	COLLEGE, UNIVERSITY	CRAFTS, TO MAKE	TO MAKE

TOUCH, ROTATE, TOUCH **CM: 31**	(BOTH HANDS) **CM: 32**	(BOTH HANDS) **CM: 33**	(BOTH HANDS) **CM: 34**
COOKIE, BUDGET	HOUSE, CAMP, TENT	CAMPING	SYSTEM, ALTAR

225

(P5) TYPE 1: FACIAL GRAMMAR

GRAMMAR BOX

T	C	WH	Y/N	RH	9

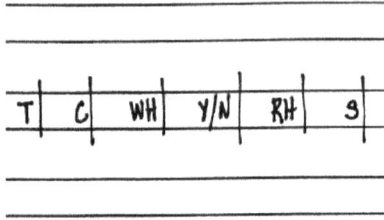

(P5) TYPE 2: FACIAL MORPHEMES

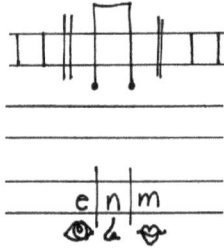

e	n	m

EYES

SQUINTY EYES	FGe: 1	FURROWED BROWS	FGe: 2	WIDE OPEN EYES	FGe: 3	EYES TRACK SIGN (SPOTLIGHT)	FGe: 4	RAPID EYE BLINKING	FGe: 5
SMALL AMOUNT, TINY		ANGRY, MAD, UPSET		THIS, OR THAT? (COMPARISON)		LOOK ON PAGE 36		BE UNAWARE OF, SERIOUSLY? THAT'S UNUSUAL...	

UPWARD GAZE	FGe: 6	DOWNWARD GAZE	FGe: 7	EYES CLOSED	FGe: 8	EYES ROLL	FGe: 9	EYE BROWS RAISED	FGe: 10
REMEMBERING, THINKING		LOOK FOR SOMETHING, GUILTY, SUBMISSIVE		IGNORING, NOT LISTENING		ANNOYANCE, OH BROTHER		Y/N QUESTIONS, PAY ATTENTION	

	FGn: 1		FGn: 2
NOSE WRINKLE: REPEATING (X2)	÷	NOSE WRINKLE: HELD	⊥
YES, AFFIRMATIVE		HUH? WHAT?	

NOSE

MOUTH

	FGm: 1		FGm: 2		FGm: 3		FGm: 4		FGm: 5		FGm: 6
OOOoo	OO	CHA	CHA	PAH!	PAH	BING	BING	ONE CHEEK PUFF	-0	PUFFED CHEEKS	0—0
LONG TIME AGO, LITTLE BIT, SMALL		LARGE AMT, BIG		FINALLY! SUCCESS!		TEND TO, TYPICALLY		CYST, LUMP		FAT, CHUBBY	

	FGm: 7		FGm: 8		FGm: 9		FGm: 10		FGm: 11		FGm: 12
FSH	Ⴤ	MMM	mm	LOWER LIP IN AND OUT	OIC	KISS	♡	LOWER TEETH EXPOSED	⊔	TONGUE HALF-OUT	⩔
FINISH, DONE, STOP IT		(DRIVING AVE SPEED) MED SIZE, AVERAGE		THAT'S INTERESTING… OH, I SEE…		KISS-FIST, LOVE IT! FAV		ACCIDENTALLY RUINED, MISTAKE		NOT-YET, AWKWARD, CLUMSY	

	FGm: 13		FGm: 14		FGm: 15		FGm: 16		FGm: 17		FGm: 18
BLOWING AIR	⊃⊂	OPEN MOUTH	⊖	TEETH EXPOSED	▭	SCHA-JAH	⌿#	RASPBERRY LIPS/BUZZ	B	BOW/POW	OW
NOTHING, WINDY		SHOCK, OBSESS OVER		BRUSH TEETH		SPEECH, SPEECH PRACTICE		BORED, OH BROTHER		SHUT DOWN, BOMB BLAST	

	FGM: 19		FGm: 20		FGm: 21		FGm: 22		FGm: 23		FGm: 24
SMILE	⩖	FROWN	⩑	TONGUE SWALLOW	≡	SHU-ZSHA	⊓∪	PTH	⊜	HALF CHEEK PULL	7
BE HAPPY, SAY CHEESE		BE SAD, UNHAPPY		ALL GONE, DISAPPEAR, GULLIBLE		MAKE FUN OF, TEASE		MELT AWAY, DECOMPOSE		RECENTLY	

	FGm: 25		FGm: 26		FGm: 27		FGm: 28
BOTH LIPS PUFFY	∞	JAW DROP	⊔	TONGUE SIDE TO SIDE, RAPIDLY	=	COVER MOUTH	⊗
COMFORTABLE, MAKE A DECISION		STUNNED, SHOCKED		WANT, HAVE TO/MUST, AWESOME, COOL		NAUSEOUS, MISTAKE/OOPS	

227

LISTING

GENERIC
LISTING

SPECIFIC
LISTING

ie: dog, cat, fish

2/2

EITHER

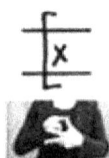

INDEX TOUCH

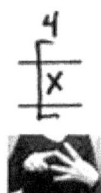

(NUMBERING)

INDEX
AIR COUNT

INDEX DRAG

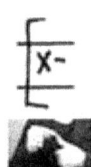

FLIP TOUCH

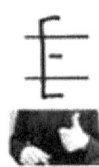

FLIP BOUNCE

VARIATION:

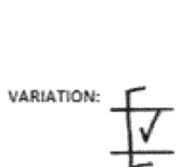

CHECK-LIST

MOUSE CLICK

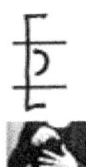

INDEX
AIR SWEEP

AIR CHOP

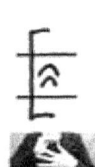

CHOP TOUCH

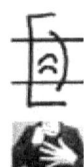

CHOP SWEEP

1ST

TWIST

AIR SPIRAL

PALM SWEEP

ASL-FIST LIST

SIGNOTATION GRAMMAR NOTES

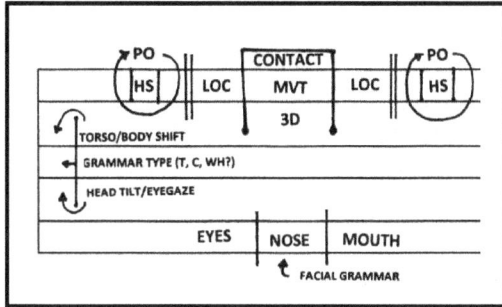

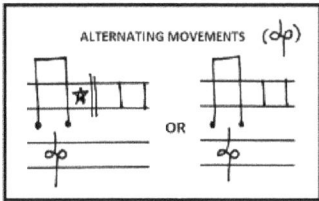

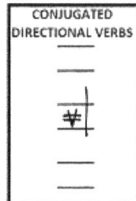

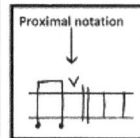

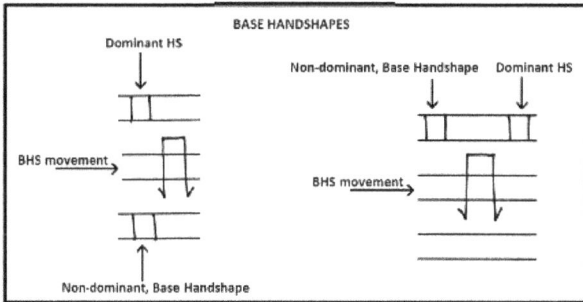

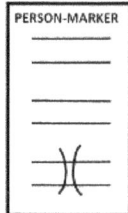

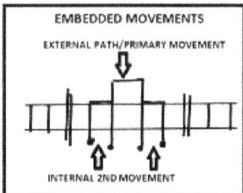

PO
HS | LOC | CONTACT MVT 3D | LOC | HS | PO

TORSO/BODY SHIFT

GRAMMAR TYPE (T, C, WH?)

HEAD TILT/EYEGAZE

EYES | NOSE | MOUTH

FACIAL GRAMMAR

ALTERNATING MOVEMENTS (αφ)

OR

MIRROR MOVEMENTS

CONJUGATED DIRECTIONAL VERBS

Proximal notation

BASE HANDSHAPES

Dominant HS

Non-dominant, Base Handshape   Dominant HS

BHS movement

BHS movement

Non-dominant, Base Handshape

COMPOUND SIGNS

PERSON-MARKER

EMBEDDED MOVEMENTS

EXTERNAL PATH/PRIMARY MOVEMENT

INTERNAL 2ND MOVEMENT

PRONOUNS

DIRECTIONALITY OF PRONOUNS

YOU	ME	HE, SHE, IT	HE, SHE, IT	YOU ALL	WE	THEY (it)	THEY (I)

INFORMAL   FORMAL

	INFORMAL	FORMAL
Personal pronoun (I, me, you, she, he, it, we, they)		
Possessive pronoun (my, your, her, his, its, our, their)		
Reflexive pronoun (myself, yourself, herself, himself, itself, ourselves, yourselves)		

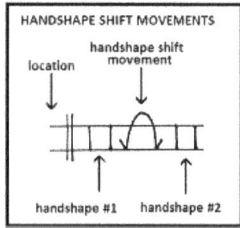

HANDSHAPE SHIFT MOVEMENTS

location   handshape shift movement

handshape #1   handshape #2

SEPARATION OF SIGNS

"yes"   "no"

ARTWORK

The artwork, sketches, photographs and notations contained in this text are the product of the author, free clip art, creative commons photos or purchased art.

DISCLAIMER

Signotation is the independent work of the author. Any resemblance to another approach or method of recording sign languages on paper is purely coincidental. This work is covered by U.S. Copyright law.

ABOUT THE AUTHOR

Shelly Hansen, CI/CT/SC:Legal/ED:K-12
has been a RID Certified American Sign Language Interpreter since 1992. She is
an active community and educational interpreter, mentor and Youtube vlogger.
Youtube channel: ASLInterpreter@S.Hansen
Contact: ASLiSHansen@gmail.com
Website: signotation.com

www.ingramcontent.com/pod-product-compliance
Lightning Source LLC
Chambersburg PA
CBHW060011050426
42448CB00012B/2707